NEMESIS

Michael Monahan

# NEMESIS

By

MICHAEL MONAHAN

*Essay Index Reprint Series*

BOOKS FOR LIBRARIES PRESS
FREEPORT, NEW YORK

First Published 1926
Reprinted 1968



LIBRARY OF CONGRESS CATALOG CARD NUMBER:
68-54362

PRINTED IN THE UNITED STATES OF AMERICA

TO

MARY HARRIMAN RUMSEY

HONORING HER DEVOTION TO ART AND HER SYMPATHY WITH THE FORWARD LITERARY SPIRIT IN AMERICA

Thou, *who never yet of human wrong*
*Left the unbalanced scale,*
*great* Nemesis!
—BYRON

# CONTENTS



## HERESIES AND AVOWALS

## THE SPHINX

## ILLUSTRATIONS

# Nemesis

## NOTICE

ACKNOWLEDGMENT is hereby made to Messrs. Doubleday, Page and Company for permission to reprint from their edition of Oscar Wilde's Works, the paper in this book entitled, "Oscar Wilde: the Retrieval."

# NEMESIS

## NEMESIS

OF all the greater figures of the old Greek mythology Nemesis has most effectually survived the Christian Dispensation. In this we mark a proof of the divine imagination of the Greeks creating an imperishable symbol of human destiny. It has been too much the fashion to regard the old pagan world as utterly without religion or Divine guidance—forsaken during some of the most wonderful ages of human history by an absentee God! No, God has never abandoned the world, and there is no more striking witness of His ordering of human affairs than is furnished by the Greek conception of Nemesis, which many centuries of the True Religion have been unable to displace. Indeed a brief study of Nemesis and her functions in the ancient pagan cult will serve to quicken the conscience of a modern true believer. I venture to give a few hints thereon for the reader's better understanding of the Title chosen for this book and its application to the subject-matter.

Nemesis was, then, in the Greek view, the Goddess of Vengeance in the domain of the human conscience, and specially charged with the punishment of acts of impiety. Her worship was immemorial, the original seat of it having been at Rhamnus in Attica, whence she is sometimes called *Rhamnusia*. Here was a celebrated image of the goddess, thirty cubits high, the work of Phidias; thus honoring her equally with Zeus and Athenae.

Adrastus, a very ancient king of Argos, built a temple to her, perhaps the first: hence her appellation *Adrastia*. In course of time Rome took her worship over, with so much else that was Greek, and her statue was placed in the Capitol—not without a profound political purpose. When the Romans were about to declare war upon any people they offered sacrifices to Nemesis in proof that their cause and intentions were just. This indeed is both ancient and very modern history.

The idea of Nemesis as an avenging power symbolizing Divine justice is familiar even to persons but little versed in the Greek Mythology. It is not so well known, even among the literate, that she was also charged with the guardianship of the relics and the *good fame* of the dead. In the pages that follow I have not consciously neglected either of her functions, yet have leaned to the milder one. If it should seem from my book that Nemesis unduly occupies herself with literary offenders the reason perhaps is because they, of necessity, carry their sins into print. . . .

O Rhamnusia, searcher of hearts, grant that I have not taken thine awful name in vain nor wrongly imputed to others the vengeance that may fall on my rash self.

O Adrastia, thou that punishest and thou that healest, pardon the errors of this weak hand and hold me not to judgment if I have rendered thee too merciful.

# BYRON—THE LAST PHASE

## I

### ASTARTE *

IN 1905 a book bearing this title ("Astarte") was published in London, the edition being limited to two hundred copies, which were mostly given to the literary press. It is now issued in an edition and at a price which make it accessible to the English-reading public everywhere, and it is become a subject of world-wide discussion. The present or second edition has been to some extent revised and re-arranged, and contains many additional letters; the whole edited by Mary, countess of Lovelace, surviving relict of the noble author. It must be allowed that she has improved the original work, and most notably by the judicious pruning of extraneous matter.

* *Astarte:* A *Fragment of Truth* concerning *George Gordon Byron,* sixth Lord Byron: Recorded by his Grandson, *Ralph Milbanke, Earl of Lovelace.* London. Christophers, Ltd.

The purpose of this large book, handsome in appearance but unlovely and repellent in its theme, is to establish the fact of a criminal intimacy existing between Lord Byron, the great English poet, and his half-sister Augusta Mary, wife of Colonel George Leigh and the mother of several children, one of whom, a girl, is declared to have been a fruit of the *liaison*. The title of the book is drawn from Byron's dramatic poem *Manfred*, and the motive of identifying Augusta with "Astarte" is obvious—a guilty passion being the burden of that poem.

This connection, illicit and incestuous, is said to have been formed prior to Lord Byron's marriage (Shelley alludes to the rumored scandal in a letter to Byron, 1816). Lord Lovelace does not allege—as did Harriet Beecher Stowe in 1869—that the guilty relation was continued *after* the marriage, and that Lady Byron was expected to acquiesce in and cover it. The author seeks to justify his revival and restatement of the charge, so shocking to human sensibilities in general and so offensive to the lovers of Byron's fame—a fame that was long regarded as second only to Shakespeare's—by pleading his obligations to the memory of Lady Byron, to which he conceives justice has thus at last been rendered.

### TRAITS OF LORD LOVELACE

Before proceeding further, it is proper to give a little attention to the author and compiler of this too "celebrated case," the son of "Ada" and the grandson of the illustrious poet. It has been alleged that there was a strain of madness in the Byron blood, and my Lord Lovelace at different times in his life gave proof of marked singularity bordering upon "queerness." Harriet Beecher Stowe met him, while still a young man, at the house of Lady Byron. She tells us, in "Lady Byron Vindicated," that she had "heard much of the young nobleman's eccentricities," and as to certain of his traits she remarked that they "might show some want of proper balance." The Earl remembered this against her when he sat down to write "Astarte"; hence his bitter and scathing references to the American woman whose offence, after all, was but to anticipate him in giving to the world the "true story" of Lady Byron and her Lord.

It would be manifestly unfair to criticize Lord Lovelace's effort from a strict literary standpoint, since he disclaimed the character and qualifications of the trained writer. But as the grandson of Byron, he doubtless felt the call to exhibit his mentality and his learning, and it may be said that the display of both—waiving the chief subject-matter of his book—would entitle it to a prominent place amongst the "Curiosities of Literature." There is, to be just, a kind of unregulated force behind it all; but the so often clotted style of his writing and the occasional perversity of his thought would never secure for Lord Lovelace a respectful hearing on literary grounds alone. This applies especially to his frequent excursions from the main theme into the domains of literature, politics, history, ethics, etc.—when it is a matter of plain narrative he handles himself tolerably well. But there are few pages wherein he "lets himself go," on which he has not stamped his singularities with a crude hand. His personalities directed against Byron's literary friends and defenders—Moore, Murray, Gifford, Wilson, *et al.*—are extremely virulent; nor does he spare Sir Walter Scott for *his* charitable view of

Byron's transgressions. At the same time he falls himself into some glaring inconsistencies, as when he extenuates the sin of Byron and Augusta by alleging the exceptional nature of their temptation * and the then prevalent laxity of morals among the English aristocracy. The same charge, he mentions, was brought against Napoleon and Shelley,† indeed a worse one, since *whole* sisters were incriminated. Another curious outburst is that where he regrets that Augusta did not fly with Byron and share his subsequent exile! Character regained he affirms to have been the consummation of her ruin and a misfortune to Lady Byron to whom, in the event of Augusta's flight, the "victory would have remained, solid and final!"

Oddities and inconsistencies of the sort here noted are never far to seek in Lord Lovelace's story and may be referable to something of that "damned crinkum crankum" which Byron humorously imputed to

* They were brought up separately, they saw little of each other in early years, and they met almost as strangers in 1812 when Byron at 24 was already in the sunburst of fame and at the height of his remarkable personal beauty.

† André Maurois, Shelley's latest biographer, admits that the poet justified carnal passion between brother and sister.

the person of his blood whom he loved best. Lovelace's avowal, seemingly unmeditated, that there was in Lady Byron a "blend of generosity, fortitude, sternness, gentleness, affection, altruism and implacability," is striking enough, for *implacable* is the first and last word that occurs to one in considering this painful history. The pen portrait of Augusta convinces by its apparent fidelity and is not disfigured by too much prejudice; on the whole, malgré the author's intent, it must be pronounced engaging, pathetic and sympathy-winning. Lord Lovelace writes: "She was a woman of that great family—often very lovable—which is vague about facts, unconscious of duties, impulsive in conduct." . . .

"She was of a sanguine and buoyant disposition, childishly fond and playful, ready to laugh at anything, loving to talk nonsense."

One is glad to see refuted the notion—first put forth by Mrs. Beecher Stowe on the claimed warrant of Lady Byron—that the woman who so fatally charmed the great poet of his age, was devoid of personal attractions. We are assured that "she was in reality a charming woman who exercised great fascination over all sorts of people in the brilliant society to which she belonged." The author points out that Augusta's portrait by Holmes, given in this edition, shows a very attractive woman—"not a regular beauty," he quaintly adds, "but one well equipped with love powder, which she knew thoroughly how to handle." She had the same father with the poet (Captain John Byron, a man of libertine and reckless character), was four years older than he, and survived until 1851. Augusta and Lady Byron remained friends—with a secret reservation, no doubt—till 1829, after which time they walked apart, as it seems, without open rupture or quarrel. But when Augusta lay dying the proud widow sent her a loving message.

Lord Lovelace exposes another curious crotchet in remarking upon the too liberal political principles of his famous grandsire. He ascribes this trait, contradictory in a man of Byron's aristocratic lineage, to the fact that through his mother he was "descended from the conquered and lawless Celts, from whom he inherited his superstitious fancies," etc. He notes that Byron spoke with sympathy of those Celtic rebels who, down to his own time, had caused so much terror and suffered such ghastly repression. He points out that in his first speech in the House of Lords Byron denounced the Union of England and Ireland as that of "the shark and his prey." It is even charged that, owing to "this infusion of alien blood," * he declined to rejoice over the triumph of the great war against Napoleon, and went into a fury on hearing of Waterloo. In "Don Juan" he lampooned Wellington, the "saviour of Europe," and ruthlessly avowed his

> ". . . plain sworn downright detestation of every despotism in every nation."

While a resident of Italy he conspired with the *carbonari* or Italian rebels against the Austrian domination. In short, this devil of a man seems to have stopped at nothing, and it must be allowed, thus variously contrived to make himself, in Macaulay's phrase, "the most celebrated Englishman of the Nineteenth century." Of all English poets, save Shakespeare, his is still the most living fame in Europe—outside of England!

Among the illustrations, two portraits of Byron

* With due respect to his very different grandson, one must be grateful, if only upon literary grounds, for the Celtic half of Byron.

are given, at twenty and twenty-six, which recall Coleridge's words: "If you had seen Lord Byron you could hardly disbelieve him—so beautiful a countenance I scarcely ever saw . . . his eyes the open portals of the sun—things of light and for light."

*The Indictment*

In the necessarily limited space at my disposal I may not attempt to examine the ill-judged and ill-advised testament of Lord Lovelace at length or in detail—this the complexity of much of the matter and its voluminous character forbid. Besides, most people will prefer to read the book for themselves—it is indeed of the sort marked out for such preference—and it is now the more readable since a large number of Byron's letters to Augusta, not heretofore published, have been added to the work—thus by a sad irony of fate making the chief charm of a book whose ostensible object is to damn him to everlasting infamy. Painful is the thought that the blood of the author of "Childe Harold" flowed in the hand that drew up this terrible accusation!

Let us see, briefly, how the indictment is presented and sustained—for alas, that it *is* sustained by the mass of testimony herein collected, so far as such a charge is in the circumstances at all capable of proof, will we fear be the judgment of most persons upon reading the book.

A long series of letters is given between Lady Byron and Augusta, than which we think more painful reading has never been offered to the public. The purpose of the unloved and aggrieved wife was to wrest a confession from the too wildly beloved sister, and her tactics to this end display an order of ability and casuistical finesse which was doubtless not inconsistent with the strictest integrity of principle. She invoked the aid of a Mrs. Villiers, an intimate friend of Augusta and quite without suspicions, to help lime the timorous creature. She agitated before the latter the spectre of social disgrace for herself and family; made much of Byron's alleged (and doubtful) incrimination of her to several persons, as well as the tendency of certain of his poems to the same effect; pleaded that she should never renew a confidential intimacy with him by letter, or any personal intercourse (there was for long a fear that Byron would return to England or that Augusta would go abroad to him); all the time pressing more and more upon Augusta her own absolute conviction of their former guilt. As a reward for compliance in these particulars, she pledged her love and friendship and agreed to maintain with her the social intimacy which was necessary to save Augusta's good name before the world. Excellent and admirable was all this on Lady Byron's part, without shadow of question, and it is perhaps but a sign of human infirmity that one's compassion is thereby strongly enlisted for the pitiful object of all this virtuous maneuvring. Well might Leslie Stephen shrink from giving his sanction to the publication of "poor Mrs. Leigh's very painful letters."

In the end the stronger brain and will prevailed; the pair met in London on August 31, 1816, and in Lord Lovelace's words, "Augusta then made full confession of the previous connection—any subsequent to Lady Byron's marriage being stoutly denied." The author adds: "Lady Byron had sometimes been inclined to think that Mrs. Leigh might have feigned resistance to Lord Byron's wishes before her and permitted them in private."

Augusta's confession, having been oral, is not given; for that we must take Lady Byron's word, but it is only fair to say that the strongest proof presumptive of it is to be gathered from the immediately sequent letters of Lady Byron, Mrs. Villiers and Mrs. Leigh herself. Henceforth Lady Byron's letters to Augusta are marked by such edifying phrases as, "Anxious as I am to sustain and comfort you in the recovered path of virtue"—rubbing it in, as it were, until one is pierced with sympathy for the hapless victim. Moreover Lady Byron not long afterwards wrote down this account of the interview referred to, for herself:

"She acknowledged that the verses ('I speak not, I trace not, I breathe not thy name') of which I have the original, were addressed to her. She told me that she had never had any suspicions of *my* suspicions except at the time, in the summer of 1815, when I evidently wished she would leave us; but she had often told him he said such things before me as would have led any other woman to suspect. He reassured her when these doubts occurred, and she seems to have acted upon the principle that what could be concealed from me was no injury. She denied that during the business of the separation he had ever addressed any criminal proposals to her. Augusta told me that she had never seen in him remorse for his guilt towards her but once—the night before they last parted, previous to his going abroad."

Subsequent to the confession Mrs. Leigh wrote to Lady Byron these most pathetic and memorable words: "Towards another person she (Mrs. Villiers) is very violent in her expressions of resentment—and it is I daresay very natural, but I think it better not to say a word in answer—tho' in fact *I am the one much the most to blame, and quite inexcusable.*"

This is the nearest she ever came to a *written* avowal of her guilt; in the view of many persons it is the one lovely thing brought to light by these unlovely disclosures, and will tell for her absolution here and hereafter.

### BYRON TO AUGUSTA

The damnatory and conclusive character of these testimonies can ill be disputed even by those who, like the present writer, are loth to receive them, save upon the strongest compulsion. But there is, the identity of the person addressed to Mrs. Musters, *née* Mary Chaworth, an early love of Byron's. This mainly on account of the short name of four letters indicated by asterisks, which was apparently effaced by the recipient. Mr. Samuel Chew, a zealous defender of the poet, has recently labored this point in order to clear Mrs. Leigh—and the present writer for one could wish that he had succeeded; but he seems unaccountably to have forgotten that her full name was Augusta *Mary*. Again, a still greater stumbling block to the Mary Chaworth hypothesis, the several letters in the text immediately following between Lady Byron and Mrs. Leigh, coinciding too in point of time, are taken up with discussing *this particular letter* and the passion expressed therein. Thus Lady Byron writes: "I have before observed to you that in the intervals of every pursuit which engaged him by its novelty, this most dreadful fever of the heart has returned. . . . This letter is an ample testimony of the prior 'reformation,' which was sufficiently evidenced to me by your own assertion . . . this impassioned, tho' as appears to me, artfully studied address to regain his ascendancy. . . . He (Byron) has not relinquished his criminal desires, and I think I may add, designs."

Finally, to the question, how did Lady Byron come into possession of this letter, there is a conclusive answer in the book before us. She had exacted a promise from Mrs. Leigh to submit all Byron's letters to herself, and the correspondence between the two women proves that Augusta yielded a full submission in this particular. And again finally, it is scarcely possible to entertain a suspicion of fraud in regard to the origin, integrity or collocation of these letters.

Thus the victory—if victory it can be called—remains to the injured wife: she took her measures with consummate care, courage and ability; she kept an inviolate silence (save to a very few intimates) during a long life; and now, at the lapse of more than a hundred years since her discovery of the intrigue, from the refuge of the grave she claims her full vindication. There will not be wanting voices to approve her course on the highest warrant of conscience, and to acclaim the result as a triumph of Providential justice. But we conceive that the world will presently be less concerned with this

LORD BYRON

question or aspect of the matter than with the ultimate effect of the scandal upon Byron's literary fame and influence. For this happily we have precedent illustrious and overwhelming, that good literature is privileged to live down the errors that so often mark the career of genius. Bacon survives the bribery impeachments and—an even worse thing—the betrayal of Essex. Shakespeare is assoiled in the blood of time from his self-accusations in the *Sonnets.* The treasure of Byron's genius remains unflawed and secure, in spite of this late attainder at the hands of his kin. Nay, the world that cherishes his undying work will rejoice in this his centennial year,* which finds his better fame still vigorously alive, that the worst is now over and done with—the long hunt of defamation at an end. In a little while these last injurious echoes are bound to die out, and we shall not then regret so much this final word of the bad legend; knowing and appraising Byron better than before; loving him not a whit the less, but making due allowance for the mixture of divine and human elements that at once made and marred him as a man and as a poet.

* The hundredth year since his death in 1824.

# THE LOVES OF SHELLEY

## I

THE world has a strong taste for moral judgments, and knowing its own frailty it is always interested in the operations of Nemesis. For these two reasons it is more concerned with Shelley the man than with Shelley the poet; in truth it has never cared much for his poetry, a few lyrics excepted. I speak of course of the general public.

Comes now a Frenchman, Monsieur André Maurois, in this centennial year of Byron, with a marvelous Life of Shelley * in which these two great and closely associated poets are made to figure like characters in a romance. The effect is to link Shelley with the Byron centenary (his own fell in 1922, being comparatively ignored), and to more

* *Ariel ou la vie de Shelley par André Maurois: Paris, Bernard Grasset.* The book has been translated, but this article takes account only of the French text.

than indemnify him for any previous neglect. Ariel and the Pilgrim seem destined henceforth to hold their immortal course together.

There have been a dozen Lives of Shelley in English, of varying merit, but not one of them compares in point of interest and artistic treatment with the Frenchman's work. Strictly regarded, however, M. Maurois's book is an innovation upon the ways of literary biographers—an utter departure from the old beaten track, the outworn stereotyped methods. What he has done, in a word, is to cast the life of Shelley in the form of a novel, but without injecting into it any element of fiction; ordering the whole, persons, incidents, documents, even conversations, with scrupulous veracity. The task was, needless to say, one of perilous difficulty that would have daunted any Englishman, and in English hands the most capable would most likely have come to disaster. Due to the unerring literary technique of the Frenchman, no less than to the genial and tolerant spirit in which the work is conceived, "Ariel" remains an achievement of high literary distinction, indeed a *tour de force* of the first order, and we may expect to see a crowd of imitations in its wake.

In France "Ariel" runs like a popular novel; my own copy dated months ago bears the stamp *55th Edition*. Such a miracle could not happen in These States, one regretfully allows, and one is almost tempted to the unpatriotic confession that 'twere better to be a literate nation, a nation of book-lovers and book-readers like the French, than to wear the self-assumed title of the "Greatest people on God's footstool!"

In what follows I shall not confine myself strictly to annotating M. Maurois's book, but shall rather supplement it, whenever needful or desirable, with information drawn from other sources. It is but fair, however, to allow that the author of "Ariel" is astonishingly accurate for a Frenchman writing upon a mainly English subject. Wherever I use M. Maurois's language I quote it, making my own translation: the reader therefore will have a care not to charge him with the present writer's reflections and observations. This caution seems not impertinent in view of the fact that the Frenchman preserves a rather more detached attitude as regards the moral questions raised by his theme—always of course in the interest of his art—than is agreeable to the Anglo-Saxon conscience (not that I regard that appendage with any deep superstition myself). His manner toward the *Advocatus Diaboli* naturally concerned in such a matter as the trial of Shelley, is the perfection of Gallic courtesy. An English commentator will not be expected to show his Sable Worship so debonair a front.

The obliging reader will also note that the title of my article limits me to a single branch of the subject, though indeed the most vital and interesting one.

## II

M. Maurois has prefixed a touching and significant motto to his book in these lines from William Blake:

> So I turned to the Garden of Love
> That so many sweet flowers bore;
> And I saw it was filled with graves.

Eros and Nemesis were in truth the divinities that ruled the fate of Shelley; through his short life ending at thirty, he was the ardent worshipper of the one and the foredoomed victim of the other. Thus his private life has for us a tragic interest, a human appeal, which we do not find in his "Prometheus" or "Cenci," however admirable these works are as poetical compositions. In truth he never planned or executed a drama so dramatic as his own life. Immersed in his Greek poets, lost in metaphysical speculations, dreaming Utopian dreams of a larger liberty, of a more rational religion, of a more benign humanity, he seemed unconscious of the tragic pitfalls which attended his footsteps and darkened his course through life. From first to last women were his undoing, yet without women he could not have been the glorious poet he was nor the man still and always beloved in spite of his errors.

Let us trace cursorily the chronicle of Shelley's love affairs, which occupies so much of M. Maurois's fascinating biography.

To begin with the earliest years, he loved his elder sister Elizabeth—*loved her too well,* it was long insisted, though I for one do not credit the accusation. It cannot be denied that he was in the habit of justifying carnal love between brother and sister—a moral condition which certainly prevailed among the Britons in Cæsar's time, but which seemed abhorrent to the England of the early Nineteenth century struggling with the subversive views released by the French Revolution. Shelley considered the theme of passionate love between brother and sister as one of the most poetic imaginable. He warmly approved the *liaison* of Lord Byron with his (Shelley's) sister-in-law Claire Clairmont *—she was not properly his sister-in-law when this connection began, as he himself, though cohabiting with Mary Godwin at the time, was not married to her, his first wife being still alive. Like his master Godwin, Shelley looked upon marriage as an odious superstition, yet when the poet put his belief into practice and eloped with Godwin's daughter, the elder philosopher was bitterly incensed. Hardly indeed would he have been reconciled to the lawless lovers but for Shelley's ready purse. More odious even than the superstition of marriage was the superstition of other people's money † in Godwin's eyes.

* Christened Jane, which name she abandoned as ugly and unsuited to her romantic disposition.

† Mark Twain points out that from first to last Shelley poured into the Skinner Street rat-hole or abode of the venerable author of "Political Justice," from eighty to one hundred thousand dollars.

To resume: Shelley loved his beautiful cousin Harriet Grove in crude, adolescent fashion, and she leaned toward him for a time, fascinated by his beauty and the charm of his personality. But she soon reverted to normal ideas as a well-bred English girl, and declined to engage herself to the atheist-liberator, even though he was heir to a baronetcy and a great landed estate. The blow almost crushed Shelley—but only for a moment! He had marvelous recuperative power, and never failed in such an event to make a quick recovery. And the cure was always the instant taking on of another passion!

He loved Harriet Westbrook (would that he had not!), and made a runaway marriage with her when he was but eighteen and she seventeen. It was one of the prettiest romances in the world—M. Maurois warms to sympathy and, almost forgetting his detachment, relates it with a charming naïveté. Harriet was the pink and perfection of little brides, golden-haired, blue-eyed and of an exquisite figure. These Babes in the Wood of romance seemed happily suited to each other. Harriet gave Shelley the uttermost love and worship of her innocent heart;

more, she yielded her mind and soul into his keeping and accepted those radical ideas which had estranged him from his family and lost him the hand of his cousin. She defended herself bravely and successfully when Shelley's most intimate friend Hogg attempted to seduce the young bride (perhaps in deference to the poet's notions of free love.) Shelley's prompt condonation of the offence is one of the hardest things to swallow in all his variegated conduct, but no doubt he felt the need of consistency in his ethical reactions. Harriet, little more than a child herself, bore the poet two children, the second a short time after his desertion of her; and little more than three years from that romantic elopement to Scotland, she was driven by Shelley's heartlessness and her consequent despair and misery to find rest in a suicide's grave. Nemesis had begun to take an active part in the affairs of Percy Bysshe Shelley.

American readers are or should be familiar with Mark Twain's "Defence of Harriet Shelley," which, by the way, is not included among M. Maurois's list of sources given at the end of his book. It is perhaps the keenest piece of critical writing to which our great humorist ever set his hand, and from its hard-pressed conclusions few normal-minded persons are apt to dissent. There is no denying it!—this is the great wound that Shelley received from life, or rather from his misreading of it and his failure or perverse refusal to live up to its holiest obligations. Our hero, the divine Poet, stands before us, pale and beautiful, the St. Sebastian of song, with that black arrow in his side, and must always so stand before the judging generations of men. Even M. Maurois, in spite of his philosophic detachment, is a little shaken in his calm and led to express himself with unwonted emotion at this catastrophe in the life of his hero. I translate—"Ariel," pp. 227–228:

> At times he asked himself if he had not been responsible, then rejected this idea with all his strength. "I have done my duty; I have always done, upon every occasion, what seemed to me the most loyal thing, without egotism or self-interest. When I left her we no longer loved each other. I provided for her liberally, according to my means, even beyond them. I did not treat her harshly. . . . Should I have sacrificed my life and my reason to an unfaithful and mediocre woman?"

His reason answered no; his friends Hogg and Peacock who surrounded him affectionately, answered no. He implored them to repeat the assurance, for, as if by flashes of interior light, he seemed to perceive a duty mysterious and superhuman in which he had failed. "In breaking traditional bonds one liberates in men certain forces unknown which then act without our being able to foresee the terrible consequences. Liberty is good only for the strong—for those who are worthy—and Harriet was a very weak soul." Again that vision of the infantile face and blond head of the drowned girl!

I permit myself a single comment on the speech above imputed to Shelley. The vindication of Harriet is clear and definitive on this point: she was never guilty of misconduct until comparatively long after Shelley had abandoned her and set up unlawful relations with another woman, to wit, Mary Godwin; when, moreover, she no longer heard from her husband and despaired of his returning to her. According to Shelley's own friends and apologists, including some members of the Godwin tribe, Harriet was intelligent, well-mannered and far from illiterate; her mediocrity of mind seems to have been a justificatory after-thought with Shelley.

And so let us turn this darkest and saddest page in the history of the loves of Shelley.

## III

I pass over the Platonic and absurd affair with Miss Hitchener, illustrative merely of Shelley's peculiar gift for getting himself involved with ineligible or undesirable females. Nor shall I dwell upon the warmer and more serious infatuation with Cornelia Turner, which caused the first coolness and estrangement between Shelley and Harriet, and undoubtedly prepared him for the bolder measures which a little later he employed with Mary Godwin.

It is clear that Ariel was, as a lover, gregarious; his fancy never could tie itself long to a single object. This was to be shown later on in respect to Mary Godwin whom he married after the death of Harriet, whom he had won and worn at the cost of so much tragedy, and whom he loved and esteemed with as much constancy as it was in his nature to give. His at first unlawful union with Mary Godwin illustrates how inextricably good and evil are intermingled in human destinies. For Mary, a deliberate accomplice in his guilt and a leading agent in the fate of poor Harriet, proved a good and faithful wife to him during the rest of his life, and after his death safe-guarded his literary bequest in a manner to secure for herself the gratitude of future generations. Something cold Mary was and with more than a hint of the unamiable selfishness of the paternal Godwin, joined to the unscrupulousness which was a broad family trait. But considering the difficulties of her position, and above all, considering Shelley the mutable, the evanescent, the intangible, the unreckonable, the irresponsible, Mary is, in the present writer's judgment, entitled to a large suffrage of esteem.

There was another inmate of that curiously assorted Godwin household, the sweet and gentle Fanny Imlay, a daughter of the first Mrs. Godwin (Mary Wollstonecraft) and issue of a love passage with a French gentleman of whom little enough is known. Less forward than the captivating Claire or the passionately designing Mary, she was no more insensible than they to the fascinations of the young poet, rebel and aristocrat in one, and the sweet poison of his eloquence. There is little doubt that she loved Shelley, the more deeply perhaps that she preserved a maidenly reserve before her idol; and Shelley himself only awoke to the truth after the sad end.

Following the elopement of Shelley and Mary to France, life became harder for Fanny in that pinched home of the Godwins where she had no right of blood and where there was little love for her. After one or two efforts to secure employment, she yielded to despair and going to a hotel in Bristol took a dose of laudanum and so ended her troubles. The elopers had seen her for a moment on their return to England; she had appeared downcast, but had given no hint of her fatal purpose. She left a pathetic, unfinished letter alluding to her unfortunate birth and her sorrowful life, and concluding in these words:

"Perhaps on hearing of my death you will feel some regret, but very soon you will have the happiness of forgetting that a creature ever existed who called herself——."

Shelley was terribly shocked by this first tragic death in his Garden of Love, especially since Mrs. Godwin hinted that it was the result of an unavowed passion for himself. He asked himself if he could ever have unwittingly encouraged such a feeling. "How difficult it is to follow the emotions of the souls of others! What sufferings one may cause without wishing it or knowing it!" These thoughts plunged him into a deep melancholy which he sought to relieve by writing a tender poem on poor Fanny —but it remains a fragment. For a greater sorrow and a darker tragedy were about to overwhelm him in the news of Harriet's death.

## IV

Mary Godwin Shelley's chief trouble with her poet-husband, dating from the first days of their connection, was on the score of jealousy. She was perpetually jealous of her *quasi*-sister Jane or Claire Clairmont, daughter of her stepmother, a young person of some beauty and charm, whose independent notions of morality did honor to the tutelage of Godwin. No careful reader of M. Maurois's book and other authorities can doubt a moment that Mary had more cause than she openly confessed. Claire was at different times an inmate of the Shelley *ménage*, whether in England or abroad on the continent, and she never made a secret of her ardent affection for Shelley. Mary prudently put the blame on her, choosing to affect a belief in the poet's invincible innocence: which did not comport well with the circumstances of her own affair with Shelley. Claire's frequent sojourns with the Shelleys were a time of torture to Mary, though the poet seemed to enjoy them greatly—indeed the pair were wont to be inseparable, as Mary complains in her Diary. Mary would stand it as long as she could, but the end always was that Claire would have to seek another shelter. After Shelley himself, his first wife Harriet, and Mary Godwin, this pert young person Claire is the most interesting character in the romance of "Ariel."

She is interesting for another reason: having flung herself at the head of Lord Byron, she became his mistress for a very short time and bore him a child, the pathetically famous Allegra, who died in her sixth year. Byron, however, never cared much for Claire, and speedily disembarrassing himself of the lady, he refused ever afterwards to see her. Milord liked to stalk his game and did not fancy a too easy conquest. Our French author acutely remarks that Shelley sought in women a source of poetic exaltation, Byron a pretext of repose. Shelley angelic, too angelic, venerated them; Byron, human, all too human, desired them, and spoke of them with contempt. "What is terrible about women," he would say, "is that one can neither live with them nor without them." And again: "My ideal is a woman who would have enough intelligence to admire me, but not enough to wish to be admired herself."

On Byron's first meeting with the Shelleys in Switzerland he had shown some kindly interest in Claire, then his acknowledged mistress, and went so far as to praise her fine singing voice and her cleverness. But as already mentioned, he soon grew tired of her, never having been much *épris* as regards this forward young person who had seduced him by post, nor would he recognize any duty on his part toward one who had flung herself at him with so much persistence. To a mild hint from Shelley that he had carried her off, he replied with a comic affectation of anger: "Carried her off? I'd like to know who was carried off in this affair, if not the poor gentleman himself. Some people accuse me of being hard towards women: all my life I have been their victim and martyr. Since the Siege of Troy nobody has been abducted so often as myself!"

There spoke a man who may never have attained the highest source of Shelley's lyrical inspirations, but who could give him "cards and spades" in all that regards the practical business of life, and it may be added, in the divination of character. Scarcely one of Shelley's so-called friends appears to the discerning reader, with the book of that life now open before him, as he appeared to Shelley himself. In certain parts of the intellect the poet reached an astonishing maturity, but in point of judgment and worldly wisdom he remained immature to the end. No doubt we touch here a chief reason why the world—the select and sympathetic portion of it—continues to love Shelley, to find excuse or palliation for his many and grievous errors, and in short to regard him, in Matthew Arnold's incensed phrase, as "a beautiful and ineffectual angel beating in the void his luminous wings in vain."

Indeed it is very difficult to bring oneself to judge Shelley harshly or even with due severity. His unconsciousness of evil motives, his nobility of temper, his unheard-of generosity to his friends, his great love of humanity and championship of the oppressed everywhere *; finally his glorious gifts and the marks of the Divine so palpably upon him, if they do not wholly convince, at least silence or weaken the voice of the moral censor.

To resume: The warm affection and devoted championship of Shelley went far to console Claire, to hearten her against the chilling repudiation of Byron, dictated as it seemed by personal dislike, and the frequent asperities of Mary. As time went by she was to have more need of the chivalrous protection which Shelley extended to her and which stood as a rock against the jealous complaints of Mary and the sneers of Byron. It was he alone who comforted her on the death of Allegra and who bore the thankless office of all negotiations with the disdainful Lord.

Throughout his skillful disentangling of these imbroglios M. Maurois is careful to abstain from moral judgments; he allows the facts to speak for

* "Me who am as a nerve o'er which do creep
The else-unfelt oppressions of this earth."
—Shelley.

themselves. Thus in regard to the relations of Shelley and Claire he reproduces, without comment, a letter from Mr. Hoppner, the British consul at Venice, to Lord Byron, in which the former charges, upon the authority of a female servant of the Shelleys, that Claire had borne the poet a son in Italy.* Byron turned the letter over to Shelley, and then upon the latter and his wife preparing a most positive and indignant denial, he claimed the right to transmit it to Hoppner, since the accusation had been made to himself. After Byron's death this letter was found among his papers. M. Maurois comments: "He had followed the course which best safeguarded his tranquillity."

Whether the accusation was true or false, and whether Mary believed it or not, she proved her good sense and strong character by repelling it with all her force and uniting with Shelley in a categorical denial. Mary knew better than to make a martyr of Claire in Shelley's eyes—that was the way to lose him!

* From his note to Hoppner acknowledging receipt of the letter mentioned above, Byron appeared to believe the charge, but Milord was only too facile in such matters, and still more indifferent.

## V

Shelley never realized, save for a fleeting interval now and then, the Ideal Woman of his dreams, but he ceased not to pursue the vision, less as we believe from the promptings of sensual desire than from a need, vital to him as life itself, of thereby fructifying his poetic thought. Almost he confesses the secret in these lines addressed to an unknown (1921):

> When passion's trance is overpast
> If tenderness and truth could last,
> Or live whilst all wild feelings keep
> Some mortal slumber, dark and deep,
> I should not weep, I should not weep!
>
> It were enough to feel, to see
> Thy soft eyes gazing tenderly,
> And dream the rest—*and burn and be*
> *The secret food of fires unseen*—
> Couldst thou but be as thou hast been.

Unrest, unappeasement is the spur of the lover and the poet, the highest potencies of both uniting in Shelley. Realising as he did the emptiness of the dream, the futility both of desire and possession, still life was not possible without it.

In many mortal forms I rashly sought
The shadow of that idol of my thought.
And some were fair—but beauty dies away;
Others were wise—but honeyed words betray;
And one was true—oh, why not true to me? . . .

I quote these lines from "Epipsychidion" for another reason—the poem was inspired by Emilia Viviani, a young and beautiful Italian lady, in whom Shelley identified his ever-sought goddess for a brief time, long enough to enable him to throw off some very fine verses. In one of these poems he confides to her:

Send the stars light, but send not love to me,
In whom love ever made
Health like a heap of cinders soon to fade.

This love,—Platonic from the circumstances, want of opportunity and the Argus-eyed vigilance of Mary,—was certainly destined "soon to fade," leaving the poet disillusioned, yet always ready for fresh illusions. Emilia presently made a rather vulgar marriage—of necessity indeed, to escape her father's tyranny—and was removed from the Shelleyan environment. Mary did not conceal her malicious pleasure. Shelley was disgusted, and could not bear to look at the "Epipsychidion." "She to whom I have been pouring forth my adoration," he said, "was a cloud and not a Goddess. It is always my error to seek in a mortal envelope the image of what is eternal."

This was the poet's last disillusion and disappointment in quest of his Idol; but he was to find the Goddess again before the end, very near yet seemingly unattainable; and once more the bird in his breast responded to the magic summons and poured forth lyric snatches of sweetest pain and ecstasy, of love's inmost longing and feigned abdication of desire, all the cunning mystery of passion sung as Shelley had never sung it before.

How Mary contained herself at sight of these demonstrations or symptoms of the malady so long familiar to her, is hard to understand, but we may be sure her self-restraint was not perfect at all points. There are many indications that the Dove of Peace was regarded as a bird of passage in the Shelley *ménage* during the last year in Italy. Shelley was writing verses about his "cold home" and looking for consolation to another home made warm and inexpressibly luring by his desire for another woman.

This woman, forever memorable as Shelley's last love, was the *soi-disant* wife of Edward Williams, a former British army officer, of some literary attainments and of amiable character, who had come to join the little English colony at Pisa. He and his wife Jane Williams were the most sincere and agreeable friends that the Shelleys had drawn to themselves in Italy. Between the poet and Williams there was speedily formed a warm attachment,* coupled on Williams's part with an immense admiration for Shelley's genius. A close intercourse was maintained between the two families, and toward the end they set up a joint *ménage* in the Casa Magni, a large and somewhat dilapidated house on the coast of the Gulf of Spezia. This

* Shelley and Williams were drowned in the Gulf of Spezia in mid-July, 1822, by the wrecking of their yacht the *Don Juan*—

> That fatal and perfidious barque,
> Built i' the eclipse and rigged with curses dark!

The best English account of this catastrophe is to be found in Trelawny's "Recollections of Byron and Shelley." In those final months Trelawny was a frequent visitor both at Pisa and Casa Magni; with Byron he conducted the cremation of the dead in the Greek manner.

arrangement soon proved irksome to Mary. At Pisa she had sought the Williamses as eagerly as Shelley himself, but now that they were all under the same roof she had a painful recurrence of her old complaint, jealousy; this time on account of Jane Williams, whom Shelley praised too much and to whom he was writing some of his finest poems.

## VI

No misconduct is alleged or even suspected on the part of Shelley and Jane Williams, but there was a tense something in the air at this time which argued that a *dénouement* was approaching. Shelley found in Jane a likeness to Antigone, whom he thought he must have loved in a prior existence. As pointed out, Jane was sympathetic and went far to humor the poet, but she was unfeignedly in love with her husband and a fond mother to their two young children. She was a pretty woman with gentle, restful manners, and possessed a beautiful singing voice. Between her and Shelley there quickly sprang up the sympathy that is the first step toward love—nay, often is love itself. She sang and her lovely voice carried Shelley far from his bitter memories and the cares of his home, which Mary, worn by child-bearing and embittered by the loss of children, did not spare him. Jane laid her cool soft hand on his brow, and he tasted a joy which Mary no longer could give him. Shelley, with his usual amazing frankness or rather his lamb-like unconsciousness of evil, was at small pains to conceal his emotions from Mary, while writing to the dear Williamses such lines as these:

Therefore, if now I see you seldomer,
  Dear friends, dear *friend!* know that I only fly
Your looks because they stir
  Griefs that should sleep and hopes that cannot
    die:
The very comfort that they minister
  I scarce can bear; yet I
  So deeply is the arrow gone,
Should quickly perish if it were withdrawn.

Surely it must have been as a sword in Mary's heart—the very sword that pierced Harriet's!—to look on at a scene which so painfully recalled the sweet and guilty past, and especially her own share in it. I wonder if she remembered then that she had not pitied Harriet?

It seems a Hibernian statement, but we must set it down nevertheless, that Shelley was never so happy as when he was miserable! By this I mean that in him an unsatisfied passion promoted that divine exaltation of spirit which found relief and expression in the finest poetry, *e. g.*, the famous lyric cry that broke from him about this time——

O world! O life! O time!
On whose last steps I climb,
  Trembling at that where I had stood before,—
When will return the glory of your prime?
  No more—oh, never more!

Or these lines unmatched for melancholy beauty:

When the lamp is shattered
  The light in the dust lies dead;
When the cloud is scattered
  The rainbow's glory is shed;
When the lute is broken
  Sweet notes are remembered not;
When the lips have spoken
  Loved accents are soon forgot.

As music and splendor
  Survive not the lamp and the lute,
The heart's echoes render
  No song when the spirit is mute.

In the last year of his life (1821–1822) Shelley wrote some of his most celestial lyrics and other poems. Jane is mentioned in several of these pieces, and I think we may feel her influence upon all. Unquestionably it was to her that he addressed the universally admired lyric in which he compared his love and longing to

> The desire of the moth for the star,
>   Of the night for the morrow,
> The devotion to something afar
>   From the sphere of our sorrow.

One can imagine what a cruel torture it was for Mary, daughter of Godwin, when at a later day she turned over these feverishly written pages, breathing love and adoration for another woman. But she proved her English mettle and her fitness to administer Shelley's literary legacy by giving to the world the poems as written, not even suppressing the name of the person addressed. Except in one instance, that of the lyric last mentioned, with its quite celestial compliment to the Beloved:—there are some things indeed which we may not ask of a woman, however Spartan-like her courage!

In after years Mary Shelley and Jane Williams

lived a long time together in London and for the most part agreed very well. Trelawny proposed to Mary, but she declined, with thanks for the honor, saying finely that she preferred the name Mary Shelley to any other. We have lately learned, however, that she made a dead set at our own Washington Irving; but the courage or enterprise of her youth failed her, and Irving proceeded in his impeccable bachelorhood, so dear to the sentimentalists of America.

Jefferson Hogg, the most ancient friend of Shelley, offered to marry Jane Williams, whereupon she owned that she had no legal right to the name, not having been married to Williams, on account of a husband somewhere in the East Indies. Thereupon, they took each other for better or worse, without priestly or legal sanction, and lived happily ever afterwards—a rare conclusion for any couple in this history.

## VII

As they grew older these ladies (including Claire Clairmont) were increasingly apt to quarrel over their joint memories and experiences. Jane having declared that Shelley had loved only herself during the last months at Pisa and at Casa Magni, Mary broke with her finally and they saw each other no more. One is pleased to learn that Jane carried into old age something of the beauty and charm which had thrilled the heart of her immortal lover.

To finish with Claire: After playing the stormy petrel during several years of Shelley's life in Italy, she relapsed into obscurity and silence from the poet's death in 1822. It is known that she planned to write a book on Shelley and Byron (a bequest from the former having secured her in a comfortable way of living), and its aim was to be moral, Claire proposing to show from her own experience that happiness could not result from a defiance of the laws of society. However, her mind weakened, as is frequently the case with persons of her extremely nervous and passionate temperament; she was forced to take a long rest, and nothing more was heard of her literary plans, for which no doubt Byron in the shades gave grateful thanks. She lived to a great age, passing her last years at Florence, having become a devout Catholic, much occupied with pious works. Toward 1879 a young man questioned her upon her recollections of Shelley and Byron. At the mention of these two famous names, a smile irradiated the old wrinkled face, recalling something of her youthful charm.

"Come now," she said, "I suppose that like all the rest of the world, you believe that I loved Byron?"

The young man only looking at her with surprise, she continued:

"My young friend, a day will come when you will better understand the heart of woman. I was dazzled by Byron, but I was not in love with him—I *could* have become so, but it did not happen."

There followed a silence; then the inquirer asked, somewhat timidly:

"So you have never loved, Madame?"

She blushed and without replying fixed her eyes on the ground.

"Shelley?" he suggested, in a scarcely audible voice.

"With all my heart and with all my soul!" avowed the old dame passionately, but without raising her eyes.

Then, with a charming coquetry, she pinched the young man's cheek. . . .

It may strike the attentive reader, as it does the present writer, that this evocation of the gadfly Claire Clairmont, pretty, wilful and passionate, a half-century after the passing of her famous lovers, gives a touch of unique interest to this true narrative, confirming Byron's observation that *"truth is always strange—stranger than fiction."*

P. B. SHELLEY

## A SEALED PAPER IN THE BRITISH MUSEUM

SINCE the appearance of Robert Hichens' "Green Carnation" many years ago, on the eve of Wilde's downfall, scandal has done Lord Alfred Douglas the dubious honor of identifying him with the "Reggie" of that brilliant pasquinade. Nay, it has gone further in the way of imputation, leaning upon certain "confessions" of Wilde himself (the most formidable and accusatory of which are sealed up in the British Museum), as also upon some allegations made by Wilde's executor (Mr. Robert Ross) and his biographer (Mr. Arthur Ransome), of the same injurious tenor.

Following a decidedly unfortunate attempt to clear his name and fame in the courts wherein, as he claims, justice was denied him, Lord Douglas seeks to vindicate himself before the public-at-large. That there was provocation for a book in the circumstances, few will dispute; whether it will procure him a clean bill of health and enable him to silence his traducers, is another matter.

Thus the "English Review" (edited by the son of Frederic Harrison) while conceding that Lord Douglas's plea forms a "document of psychological interest," observes at the same time that the author's "pontifical moralizations and denunciations of modern tendencies are not likely to be taken seriously," adding that "quite apart from the Wilde controversy, Lord Alfred Douglas has a public record difficult to bring in harmony with the display (in this book) of conscious saintliness."

It has been freely intimated that the Douglas's book has no sort of significance save to literary garbage hunters nosing the last offal of the Wilde nuisance. But this is unfair both to the intention and the execution of the work, however much to be regretted on other grounds. The book is keenly interesting and tense with challenge:—in view of the bitter legacy of fights and litigations which Wilde has bequeathed him, it is not surprising that the noble author should seem always in a chip-on-shoulder, Marquis of Queensberry attitude. One feels that the Douglas is a man of pluck and spirit, and one cheerfully grants him the hearing which is due to these qualities.

The Douglas has plenty to say for himself and more than enough to say against his old comrade, whose charm and fascination nevertheless he freely admits. I think he is most interesting when he is not abusing or depreciating Wilde, which is in truth but seldom. This suggests what seems to me the capital error of his performance; had he pitied the dead man more and denounced him less, he would have made sure of a far greater measure of public sympathy, and this seemingly magnanimous utterance would stand a fair chance of being accepted at its full value:

"Truly if any man has had cause for tears and bitter regrets I have had cause. All my life, from twenty years of age up, has been overshadowed and filled with scandal and grief through my association with this man Oscar Wilde. I am not going to shed public or private tears about it, and I am not going to waste my breath in vain regrets. I have absolutely an easy conscience as regards my treatment of Wilde both before and since his death. If I have hurt anybody at all, it has been myself and my family, and I have done this only through misplaced loyalty to my friend and a too high regard for chivalry."

Undoubtedly the sensitive nobleman wrote this book with his own hand, and its nervous, crepitant style is admirably suited to the subject-matter. It must be allowed that the Douglas possesses no mean literary gifts for a Lord—was he not editor of the London "Academy"?—and has heretofore written passingly well both in verse and prose. Indeed his versatility suggests some of Wilde's *tours de force,* such as the composition of poems both in English and French. It was the patter of the disciple maybe, and the echo was never to be mistaken; but *néanmoins,* the talent was undeniable. I have a book of these poetical efforts and they are no discredit to the literary genius of either tongue. (Perhaps I am in error in imputing the French version to his Lordship, but the title-page bears no other attribution.) The Douglas was young when he wrote these poems and he vaunted much of the "splendid sins" which are the best appanage of youth, according to the philosophy of his master. But the finest fruit of his Lordship's talent that I am acquainted with is a Sonnet on the death of Oscar Wilde. It proves him to be a true poet—would that we might add, a loyal and magnanimous friend!

I dreamed of him last night, I saw his face
All radiant and unshadowed of distress,
And as of old, in music measureless,
I heard his golden voice and marked him trace
Under the common thing the hidden grace,
And conjure wonder out of emptiness,
Till mean things put on beauty like a dress,
And all the world was an enchanted place.
And then methought outside a fast-locked gate
I mourned the loss of unrecorded words,
Forgotten tales and mysteries half said,
Wonders that might have been articulate,
And voiceless thoughts like murdered singing birds;
And so I woke and knew that he was dead!

This touching and beautiful tribute to his friend is in violent disaccord with the note of Lord Douglas's "vindication," which is supported by a meticulous and unsparing attack upon the dead man —his looks, his personal qualities, his social pretensions, his family antecedents, his morals, his manners, his poetry, his prose, his plays—hatred has left nothing out of the account. And all this elicited by the threat of that sealed manuscript in the British Museum!

A sad and rather unworthy thing about these *amantium iræ* is that the parties charge upon each other the waste of much moneys, and cheque-stubs are brandished as freely as other weapons more proper to literary warfare.

And so the splendid sins of our youth become the grey sorrows of our middle age!

## II

Lord Douglas banks on his rank and title overmuch, with special regard perhaps to his American audience. He frankly says—we do not like him the less or dislike him the more for it—that "one cannot be the son of the eighth Marquis of Queensberry nor a member of the family of Douglas without having the defects of one's qualities."

He dedicates the work to his mother, the Dowager Marchioness of Queensberry, and there are portraits of the late Marquis (who made all the trouble), Oscar Wilde, the author himself, his wife,

Lady Alfred Douglas and their young son. The portraits of Lord Alfred go to prove that the legend which imputed good looks to him as far back as the "Green Carnation" days, was not without specious warrant. There is a marked suggestion of Wilde's Narcissus-like heroes in the perhaps slightly idealized drawing of the Douglas at the age of twenty-four. It is the face of a poet as spiritualized as Shelley—the poet, we should say, who wrote that unforgettable Sonnet on his dead friend.

The large frontispiece portrait prefixed to this book exhibits his Lordship as a handsome man of early middle-age, with a certain mingled hardness and pathos of expression. The eyes are very fine and the mouth has a beauty of its own, though with a hint of tragedy. Somewhere—somehow, I suspect my Lord Douglas has met the Furies. Remains to be said that there is nothing about any of his portraits to instigate prejudice or procure a verdict against him.

In spite of the too often harsh and embittered note of the book, it is relieved by many light touches, fortunate flashes of mundane sense or criticism, and frequent ebullitions of the fighting spirit of the author. There are appetizing glimpses of the literary and social London that Oscar Wilde loved but too well, and the exhibition lacks neither wit nor malice. Here and there one seems to catch something of the personal charm which long fascinated even the captious esthete. I offer several random extracts showing the author's capacity for shrewd observation and a turn for epigram which at this late day need not be ascribed to his paradoxical master.

He (Wilde) always struck me as being garbed in perpetual readiness to walk out or dine out with the duke or prince of the blood who would one day surely be calling round for him. . . .

The Wilde of my time consisted, to a great extent, of silk hat, frock coat, striped trousers and patent leather boots. Add to these a very tall clouded cane with a heavy gold knob and a pair of grey suede gloves, and you have the outward man. . . .

With women Wilde succeeded a great deal better than with men. Somehow, the men made him either very stiff or very limp. His bow was wasted upon them and his diffident attempts at epigrams missed fire. . . .

I believe that at the bottom of his heart Wilde felt that his true genius had found expression in his plays. . . .

He was not even anxious to be known as a poet in the way that some of his contemporaries were anxious to be known. He told me that to be dubbed "poet" was to raise up visions of untidy hair, dirty linen, and no dinner to speak of; and such a view of himself he abhorred. . . .

That Wilde had a good, easy prose style and did at times write accomplished prose I admit; but he lacked a kind heart just as surely as he lacked a coronet, and Norman blood was as alien to him as simple faith. . . .

Wilde was wont to describe himself not only as a Lord of Language but as the King of Life. . . . The King of Life business has always appeared to me to have been settled at the Old Bailey. . . .

Like most Irishmen, he was troubled all his life with attacks of regret which he was accustomed to call remorse. He believed that he had supreme gifts and that he had squandered them. . . .

He would bemoan his wasted life and come very nigh shedding tears about his shallowness at ten o'clock in the morning; while at one o'clock on the same day he would be swallowing ortolans as if they were oysters and swearing over some silly liqueur that he was the greatest genius that ever lived. . . .

The marvel of it was that he never became really drunk, though from four o'clock in the afternoon till three in the morning he was never really sober. The more he drank the more he talked, and without whisky he could neither talk nor write. . . .

Wilde was too keen an artist to allow anybody or anything to come between him and what he would call a realizable mood. The truth is that he would begin to write with great zeal and fury and apply himself to it and to the contemporaneous consumption of cigarettes and whiskies till he became utterly exhausted. . . .

Wilde once said to me when we were discussing poetry that there were two ways of disliking poetry —one being to dislike it and the other to like Pope. . . .

In naming his book "Oscar Wilde and Myself," Lord Douglas selected a title that accurately denotes the work, for Wilde remains the hero of the performance and, contrary to the author's intent, sympathy somehow pursues him to the end. Hence I suspect the Douglas erred by his "omnibus" denunciation and repudiation of his dead friend, as also by the invidious attacks upon his literary fame and credit. It is not easy to reconcile the latter animus with his claim, unproven as it must be in the circumstances, that "Wilde consistently made free use of such gifts as I possessed, that I assisted him to many a piece of dialogue and many a gibe which has helped to make him famous, and that I gave him very material aid and counsel in the matter of the *Ballad of Reading Gaol.*"

Here he ingenuously states the reason for his belief elsewhere expressed, that the "Ballad of Reading Gaol" is the one literary work of its author which seems destined to reach posterity!

Lord Douglas rather frequently alludes to his own poems and other literarv efforts, which I fancy will be puzzling to most readers, since it may be said, without ironical motive, that his Lordship's fame is no-wise commensurate with his ability. But again I think he errs in contriving once or twice to suggest a comparison between his own work and that of Wilde, which shall be favorable to himself. Even the friendliest and most impartial reader will not go with him so far.

Once more, he makes too much of the note of immorality or if you please, *un*morality, in a great part of Wilde's writings. I fear the casuistry of middle age has jaundiced his Lordship's view of the matter, impelling him to utter so harsh a judgment as this:

"He preaches always (flatly or by innuendo) that vice is at least more interesting than virtue; that insincerity is better and more to be desired than truth; that cynical carelessness and indifference are more comely than kind feeling and altruism; and that the whole end and aim of life is to eat delicately, sleep softly, and be wicked and depraved as you like, provided that you are wicked and depraved in a graceful manner."

I have known many persons who failed to derive so evil a precept, or indeed any harmful notion, from the writings of Oscar Wilde, and even Lord Alfred Douglas himself once upon a time gave testimony that he *"wrote on the side of the angels."* But hatred has changed all that—and the sealed manuscript in the British Museum!

## III

Finally, as I have already suggested, it is much to be doubted if this *apologia* of the Douglas will avail to remove the blot from his escutcheon. The putting forth of this audacious book in which so many people's corns are trampled upon, seems to me an ill-advised proceeding, in view of all the circumstances of that disastrous friendship. Let us see how the issue stands.

On page 85 of the book under review, Lord Douglas says:

"My father had accused Wilde of certain abominations. These accusations it seems were true. Wilde denied the truth of them to me and proceeded to take up what in view of the facts known to himself and not to me, was a ridiculous prosecution against my father. He was, of course, beaten, and the authorities turned upon him and convicted him of crimes which he had denied. Then I became a convenient scapegoat."

His Lordship further states and avers on pages 169 *et seq.*:—

"Any one who knows me must be well aware that when it came to the question of his (Wilde's) ultimate vices, such influence as I had over him was on the side of goodness and decency rather than otherwise. In all his cunning, overweening and merciless desire to damage and destroy me, Wilde could never find it in his heart to set down the last unthinkable lie. He knew that if he did he would be blankly sinning against the Holy Ghost; and hate me as he would, rage as he would, he could not bring himself to bear the terrible risks. Nowhere in all this outpouring of hate does he dare to come out with the accusation which would put me outside the pale of social possibility. That he was quite willing to have shouted that accusation out at the top of his voice, if there had been the slightest ground for it, is only too evident from the general drift of what he has to say."

If the accusation was not made (or intimated) which would put Lord Douglas beyond "the pale of social possibility" where then, the reader will naturally ask, were the need of 306 pages of self-vindication?

The answer to this is to be found in the Wilde MS. locked up in the British Museum and not to be made public until 1960, when perhaps people will be less concerned about the matter than they are now. But posterity will not receive the prurient bequest intact: some portions of the withheld manuscript were permitted to be read in the libel proceedings brought by Lord Alfred Douglas against

Mr. Arthur Ransome, biographer of Wilde (referred to above). The effect on judge and jurors of such reading was to secure a summary verdict of acquittal for the defendants.

So far as I am informed, the inviolable character of the Museum MS. was generally respected by the English newspaper press. At any rate, I have been unable to procure any version or even part version of it in an English publication. Lord Douglas explicitly states that he is forbidden to quote from the Museum Manuscript in the work before us.

However, that enterprising publication, the *"Mercure de France,"* being outside the pale of British jurisdiction, managed to obtain and published a very large portion of the "secret" document. I quote from this, making my own translation.

"The sins of another were charged to my account. Had I wished to do so, at both trials, I could have escaped at the expense of this other, sparing myself, not the shame certainly, but the imprisonment. . . .

"I could have left the court room with my head high and my hands in my pockets, free! In urging me to do this the greatest pressure was brought to bear upon me. I was fervidly exhorted, prayed and supplicated to adopt these tactics by people who had no other care than the good of me and mine; but I refused, I did not wish to do this thing. Even during the bitterest hours of my imprisonment I have never for a single instant regretted my decision. Such conduct would have been beneath me.

"The weaknesses of the flesh are nothing: they are maladies the cure of which is left to the doctors, if indeed they are curable. Only the weaknesses of the soul are degrading. To have obtained my acquittal by such means would have been a torture for the rest of my life.

"But do you really believe that you were worthy of the love I then testified for you, or that I ever for a single instant judged you worthy of it? I knew that you were not. But love does not haggle in the market place or use the huckster's scales. Its joy, like the joy of the intellect, is to feel itself alive. The end of love is to love—neither more nor less. You were my enemy, an enemy such as no man has ever had. I had given you my life, and in order to satisfy the lowest and most contemptible of human passions—hate, vanity, covetousness—you had wasted it. In less than three years you had completely ruined me in every way."

Against this terrible witness of the dead, which is explicit and damnatory enough for the least prejudiced mind, Lord Alfred Douglas's sprightly and malicious and very readable volume of over three hundred pages, would seem to weigh as light as thistledown. Unfortunate that it should be so, but so it is. I repeat, he had been a wiser man had he trusted to time and his Sonnet to vindicate him, or at least give him the benefit of the doubt—of which the present writer would not willingly seek to deprive him.

In fairness to Lord Douglas his own deliberate answer to this evident incrimination of himself in the Museum MS. is here given:

"If a friend had been involved in the slightest way, that friend's name would most assuredly have leaked out in the course of the proceedings; and if twenty friends had been involved and their names had been kept secret, Wilde's position would not have been bettered in the slightest degree or his guilt any the less plainly established. Wilde was not of the stuff that goes to hard labor with the name of a friend in his bosom when, by mentioning that name, he could have cleared himself. His whole principle of life was subversive of any such high altruism; he would not have gone without his dinner to save a friend—much less have faced ruin and imprisonment."

Let us make an offering to Nemesis, the stern deity who is not to be propitiated by youth or beauty, genius or fame, or even the nobility of the son of the eighth Marquis of Queensberry! Surely she has never wrought anything more sad and more ironical than this latest and, it is to be hoped, final chapter in the legend of Oscar Wilde.

# OSCAR WILDE: THE RETRIEVAL

## I

FITLY enough, the paradox pursues Oscar Wilde even after death—there is something paradoxical in his surviving fame, in the conditions and circumstances of his literary retrieval. As everybody knows, with the social anathema pronounced upon him in 1895, the man and the writer underwent a well-nigh complete occultation; for several years thereafter,—or virtually until his death in 1900,—little was heard of him who had "blazed the comet of a season." The publishers were "shy" of his books or even ostentatiously repudiated them in deference to public clamor, and his delightful plays were absolutely withdrawn from the theatre. Philistinism scored a thumping victory over its most redoubted foe—but it was not to hold, as we have seen.

The remark as to the interdict on his plays is more especially true of the theatre in England, where Wilde had incurred condemnation and sentence as a moral scapegoat; but the ostracism of poet and playwright was hardly less drastic and effectual in this country. On the European continent, however, Wilde's plays were never denied a hearing (Paris went to see and applaud "Salome" while he was still in prison), and it must be allowed that his complete literary rehabilitation began with foreign sympathisers.

How far and how wondrously this has proceeded is now known of all men. Since 1900, within twenty years of his death, many editions of his books (too hastily assembled in not a few instances) * have been brought out here and in England, and they have been made accessible to foreign readers through numerous translations. In the foreign theatre, as more tardily upon the English

* In certain of these publications a large quantity of matter is put forth as Wilde's which has since been repudiated by his literary executors. Also too much of his negligible work, mere journalism for the most part, has been preserved, with the aim of swelling the general contents. Doubleday, Page & Company have lately put forth what may fairly be called a *definitive* edition of Wilde.

and American boards, his plays may be said to have renewed themselves and to have acquired a classical tenure. The race for immortality is a long one, subject to gusts and flaws of public caprice, and other untoward accidents. But the odds are upon Wilde at present, even to the prejudice of his more renowned model and predecessor:—whatever reproach may lie in the matter, "Lady Windermere's Fan" and "An Ideal Husband" are far more frequently acted nowadays than the "School for Scandal" and "The Rivals." Oscar has indeed "come back" with an *éclat* and a fulness of triumph that would have astounded his none too self-depreciatory spirit.

How was the wonder accomplished, or to come nearer the heart of the matter, what was the quality in the man and in his work (for in this regard they are identical) that enabled him to set aside the social attainder, mollify or placate the terrible Mrs. Grundy, and win back to his lordship of the theatre, while at the same time retrieving his now freely conceded and distinguished place in English letters?

I will say it in one word: it was *charm,* the compelling talisman of Oscar Wilde's genius.

Much has been said in and out of print regarding the Christian magnanimity of the public in taking this flagrant sinner to its bosom again, after showing him very thoroughly what it could do in the way of chastisement and reprobation. It is a sort of unctuous self-gratulation which the public likes to indulge in when the periodical "spasm of virtue" has passed, and it wishes to put a good face on the consequent revulsion; when it takes to its arms again, with a redoublement of passionate fondness, the idol that it rejected yesterday with killing scorn and hatred. But as I conceive, one may with a good conscience decline to flatter the public sensibilities in the present instance. The reversal of its attitude toward Wilde seems to me very much less the effect of Christian magnanimity in itself than of literary charm in the offender. The public is not always a fool (this is truth, not flattery!), nor can it be fooled, as hath been illustriously stated, "all the time." Wilde had that to give which it could not or would not permanently put by.

And so a truce to all the homilies that have been

preached or printed on this matter. Good literature has the privilege of living down a bad reputation—and the reader may trust me that Wilde's "character" is not the worst that might be cited to the point. One may not wish to hold with Carlyle that literary annals offer us a sort of Newgate Calendar, but neither is it proper to regard them as a species of *Acta Sanctorum*. After all it is now justly felt that the heaviest part of Wilde's offending was against himself, while he paid full penalty with a ruined career and a life cut off in its creative prime. Sophisticated as the man not seldom appears in his formal *apologia*—which is yet not without high spiritual value and a due sincerity—he was also, paradoxically, a great simple. Something of the saint even shines out in his authentic confessions,* though both reader and penitent are now and again distracted by the artful beauty of the

* The literature that has gathered about Wilde is extraordinarily copious, including several full-length lives, numerous memoirs and sketches, critical studies, "vindications," *personalia* of every species. One or two ambitious attempts have been made to "confess" him (lacking warrant from Wilde himself), but without raising the question of motive or veracity in these instances, it suffices that they have not been accepted by the right-feeling and right-judging public. *De Profundis* is the last word on this subject.

phrase, the perversely poetical turn or trope, the preoccupation of the inevitable artist even when the man honestly strove to bare his very soul. Nevertheless, as has been said, his expiation paid for all: —*that* was indeed as plenary and tragic as the Greek conscience would have exacted. In later days when he wrote *De Profundis* (which was not published during his life) he may have been and doubtless was anxious to repudiate this view of himself as being too shockingly at variance with his long maintained pose of a careless poet and dilettante—one who, like Heine, had even demeaned himself as a pagan god, "laughing cheerfully down upon dismal Nazarenes!" But the picture has its deep-seated truth all the same, and it helps us to understand the man behind his various antic masks. That he must always remain much of an enigma, even to the most penetrating study, is quite true; Wilde himself could not have given the solution.

## II

Happily our present business is rather with the poet, the wit, the master of prose comedy, the delightful critic of literature and manners, the Great Fantastic, the Prince of Talkers, the Oscar Wilde who won his first public recognition with a smile, and who is now fully restored to his smiling dominion over English readers. His sins, though they were scarlet, have been washed white in the blood of time; and it were a morbid casuistry that would further occupy itself with or seek to draw the public attention upon that regrettable phase of the man.

He belongs, as I have already suggested, to the Race of Charmers—a very select and distinguished *corps* in the literary republic. Some of the greatest writers—the fames most enduring and marmoreal —are not perhaps to be included amongst them (one would not advisedly call Milton or Dante *charming;* applied to these mighty sovereigns of song the word seems to have a diminutive effect). But the charmers have this enviable and peculiar distinction:—the world's favour goes out to them in most spontaneous and liberal measure, for by virtue of charm they compel their own acceptance. They are the petted darlings of the minor Muses—(if one may venture to discriminate among the Immortal Nine) who have indemnified them with an extra portion of cuddling and sweetness for their inability to achieve the supreme heights of poetry. Let us instance two remarkable examples, one from either side—Goethe and Heine. Nobody would raise the question as to which is the greater poet and literary artist, the creator of *Faust* or the singer of the *Intermezzo;* nor I conceive would any person of just discernment deny that Heine is the greater charmer. This is even more evident if we draw into the comparison their prose works, such as "Wilhelm Meister" and the "Florentine Nights": charm in fuller measure and of more seductive quality must certainly be ascribed to the latter and slighter performance.

But what, then, is charm, the reader here puts in, chafing under these didactics; and this gives us pause, for it has been defined as variously and unsatisfactorily as poetry itself. Howbeit, we hazard this definition of our own—(at least we have not consciously borrowed it):—Charm is the emanation of the grace of personality through literary expression, the quintessence of genius and character, the peculiar ingratiating appeal of the soul of the writer to the soul of the reader. In a word, charm is from the Graces, a divine gift; and the writer that has it can no more be neglected, for long, than the woman who possesses beauty.

Oscar Wilde had charm in a quite un-English degree, which is readily understood from the fact that he was born with a clear title to the blarney-stone as an important item of his patrimony. Wit and humour delicately discriminated, and a certain individual smiling "hubris," that always came gracefully short of insolence, made up the Wildean charm from the first. Very early in his career he added to these qualities, Paradox—which thereafter became the chief god of his idolatry and maybe, as is the wont of such o'erweening worship, urged him later on to some unwise extremes both of precept and practice. Wherever he stopped in his careless yet purposeful way, he left men laughing and admiring—by the same token also women, who yielded even more readily to his charm and helped him to make his undeniable conquest of Belgravia, or the higher English society. For more than with Poetry, more than with Prose, more than with Plays, more than with Paradox itself, he was concerned with *Oscar Wilde,* with the artistic projection of his admirable self—"all art being (in his own language) a mode of acting, an attempt to realize one's personality on some imaginative plane out of reach of the trammelling accidents and limitations of real life."

More successful than Balzac's *Lucien,* he became the spoiled favourite of society, which was meanwhile sitting to him for his plays, polished and perverse, yet sufficiently authentic in their dramatization of fashionable manners. The legend of his social success, of his triumphs as a talker or rather monologuist in the great houses of London, is still more interesting to us than any work of his pen.* This part of his life no doubt appeared to Wilde as a veritable Field of the Cloth of Gold; we know indeed that the bitter recollection of it in his last years condemned him to literary sterility. In this brilliant sphere, stimulated by the admiring attention and applause of England's *élite,* Wilde found at times fresh sources of talent in himself and out-

* Wilde confessed to André Gide, not long before the end, that he had "given his genius to his life but only his talent to his writings"—something more than a half-truth.

did all tradition as an incomparable talker. It is allowed that he shone without a rival; men of talent, his literary competitors, submitted to his delightful tyranny of talk: they might disparage his essays, scout his plays as tinsel and *pastiche,* sneer at his Greek and set him down as a third-rate poet; but there was no denying or belittling the nightly triumphs of the *improvisatore.* But the picture so splendid and alluring had its dark side, and the artist had to pay a price for his wonderful success. His elation did not carry over to sober work-a-day hours. In these tourneys so flattering to his vanity Wilde engaged resources of talent and thought which he was never able to retrieve for the printed page.

In a sort of actor's guise he first presented himself to the public, disarming censure with his youth and debonair self-possession, and when need was, taking the sting out of coarse buffoonery, humiliating his parodists and burlesquers with refined yet telling malice. All this was charming, besides, and I am one who would not give up the Sunflower period and the American Lecture Tour for some later and more admired passages of his career. These early projections of the Oscarian personality, these none too timid tentatives of the Poet as Mime, above all, these adventures of the Humourist, were attended with some literary results which even at this late day seem fully to justify them. The long interval has not robbed these Lectures, Impressions, Notes, etc., of their wittily impertinent appeal, nor has it appreciably dulled the Wildean flash and sparkle. It was characteristic of the man, with his horror of the beaten path, that instead of "doing a book on America," like so many of his ill-advised predecessors from the other side, he merely embodied some airily satirical, not unkindly, and of course paradoxical observations upon our ways and our manners, that can still be read with relishing enjoyment. It may be pointed out that as an international character he furnished more gayety and of a wittier sort than any contemporary rival or co-attraction. In this respect also he succeeded in making a distinctly individual impression. Genius will always bring something new, says Balzac. There was at least a specious novelty about Wilde's earlier approaches to fame.

## III

Remark also that Wilde had a genius for success —the greatest of a great man's qualities, according to Thackeray, and from the outset he was never fastidious about the means of procuring it. He was a true child of his period, and his period was that of the author who "consents to be interviewed," or does not baulk at interviewing himself. To his intimates he liked to quote the old Latin adage, that fame begins in a man's own house. First of all he proposed to succeed, and rightly he felt that the direct way lay in action. All his seeming extravagances, the sunflower-and-lily craze, the public and private histrionism, the early vagaries of costume and the later conventional dandyism, the poetical long hair and the Neronian coiffure, the epigram, the paradox, the society monologue or improvisation,—were consciously directed to this end. He was in truth, as we say now, a marvellous self-advertiser; but the characterization, it should be noted, implies less reproach at present than it did when Oscar set forth conquering, and to conquer. So many great men since Wilde's heyday—to say nothing of the "near-great"—have taken a leaf out of his book or familiarized us with a variant of his methods that we are become incurably skeptical as to the once accredited union of talent and modesty! However, it is agreed that while Oscar has had many sedulous apes and understudies in the art of *Réclame,* he has never had, artistically regarded, an equal or even a good second. And one must aver—perhaps with a sting of private compunction—that it is not the least attractive part of his legend.

*Qualis ab incepto* is the Horatian word, and one is almost tempted to put forth the heresy, that successes are born—not made, *malgré* the didactics of Samuel Smiles and that ilk. At any rate Oscar seems to have had but one unqualified failure, the prose tragedy of *Vera,* dealing with Russian Nihilism, a work of his 'prentice hand. Something might be said in mitigation of this dramatic misfire, were it not of slight consequence. Charm floated him triumphantly over all the rest. Even his first book of poems succeeded brilliantly, in spite of the critical depreciation with which it was received; in spite, too, of the fact—natural enough

OSCAR WILDE

in a young man's virgin effort—that it was here and there almost clamantly "echoful," with a quite donnish ostentation of academic learning; and, finally, that it had too much to say about the Greek Eros, and too little reserve in putting the same.

But there was fine promise and not a little genuine performance in this first book—in fact certain of the poems are curiously mature and strike perhaps as high a note as Wilde ever registered. There was no remarkable precocity about this literary début in 1881. Wilde was then at the sufficiently ripe age of twenty-seven (Byron was three years younger, it will be recalled, when he "awoke one morning and found himself famous"). It is also interesting to note that this first published collection of Wilde's verses (I pass by *Ravenna,* the Newdigate prize poem, put forth in 1878) contains the major part of his poetical writings. *The Sphinx, the Ballad of Reading Gaol,* and *The Harlot's House* were, I believe, his only important poems written or published thereafter.

Bearing this in mind, his early withdrawal from poetical effort and the diversion of his mature powers to other forms of composition, one is justified in setting a higher value on his first Poems than the contemporary critics would have allowed. There were rare and unforgettable things in the book, unfeigned passion, the lyrical escape of high emotion, the bravery and challenge of no common spirit, that proclaimed the true poet. I may instance such pieces as the famous introductory sonnet *Hélas*—

> To drift with every passion till my soul
> Is a stringed lute on which all winds can play;

the sonnet of like motive, *Tædium Vitæ*—

> To stab my youth with desperate knives, to wear
> This paltry age's gaudy livery;

the *E Tenebris* (most quoted of all Wilde's poems)—

> Come down, O Christ, and help me! reach thy hand,
> For I am drowning in a stormier sea
> Than Simon on thy lake of Galilee;

the sonnet for Easter Day, beginning,

> The silver trumpets rang across the dome;

the *Rome Unvisited,* which was honoured with Cardinal Newman's praise, and the *Panthea* ever memorable for this exquisite verse—

So when men bury us beneath the yew
Thy crimson-stainéd mouth a rose will be,
And thy soft eyes lush bluebells dimmed with dew;
And when the white narcissus wantonly
Kisses the wind its playmate some faint joy
Will thrill our dust and we will be again fond maid and boy.

These poems, to mention no more, will occur to every reader as making good Oscar Wilde's claim to the laurel, and moreover as suggesting what he might have done in poetry had he devoted his life to it. But here again we must allow for the interposition of those Fates which provide for the destiny of exceptional men. Viewing Wilde's literary achievement,—very considerable as a whole,—it is perhaps not to be regretted that he left us but one book of poems—we know that it is and will be the more cherished on that account. Thrice happy among the sons of Cadmus is he who writes but one book and that a true one!

Finally Wilde snatched an immortal success from

the very ruin and shipwreck of his life, giving us in the *Ballad of Reading Gaol* not merely the most remarkable poem of its kind in English literature, but voicing a challenge to our deepest sympathies, to the very God within us, that will not be silenced until some sensible image of Christ-like justice shall have been secured for the outlawed Pariahs of the race. It is the best fruit of Wilde's talent—indeed the one work of his that has united all suffrages. There are not a few men of good repute in the world's ear who would gladly take Wilde's punishment for the glory of that Poem. Compensation is understood of the gods alone.

## IV

Wilde has been dubbed "an artist in attitudes"; pose and artificiality became, as it were, a second nature to him: which mask repels many readers and prevents their doing justice to his essential genius and originality. At any rate, his pose is his own; he imported an accent into literature which is not easily mistaken for that of another. Of dulness he was never accused; every page of his writing, even his mere journalism, detains us. All told, he was a pretty equal workman and a versatile: one hardly knows where to look for a lighter, suppler hand, a more graceful "attack," an art more suave or a more demurely ironical method than Wilde exhibits in his essays, novelettes, short stories, etc. I may cite *The Canterville Ghost* and *Lord Savile's Crime* as examples of a frolic, fantastical humour, a capacity for delicious fooling joined to a fertile invention and an unstaled manner, which one would vainly ask of the bright young authors of the present hour who regard Wilde as "outmoded." His prose Fables—poetry in all respects save form—are curiously distinct and removed from his other writings. In these unlaboured fancies, which have a charm for young and old alike, he has made proof of the eternal innocence of the artist. True it is, however, that in the literary essays proper, the Decay of Lying, the Poet as Artist, etc., Wilde makes something too much of his besetting passion for paradox, with the result that, humour him as we may, the argument is sometimes difficult to follow, and what is worse, the entertainment threatens not to come off; happily this disaster never actually occurs. I know some persons, and not of the least appreciative sort, who profess to make hard work of reading the *Intentions*—for cleverness carried too far repels us almost as much as its opposite. Then it must be allowed that Wilde sins against taste in his somewhat invidious display of "literature," never Englishing his foreign or classical quotations, putting all his goods in the show window, as it were, and exposing a "front" that is bound to challenge the spirit of irony. He is as profuse of Greek as Kipling was formerly of Anglo-Hindu, and it is evident that he cannot keep Oxford out of his thoughts. On the other hand, this parade of Oscar among the learned humanities has its delightful and profitable side, while it is relieved of pedantry by the quickness of the transitions and the unfailing *verve* of the lecturer. And how much he gives us from that full-freighted memory of his; what solid values, too, that offset the glancing paradox and the sophisticated theme! Now and again you shall come across a piece of prose like coloured mosaic or curious arabesque, hardly to be matched in Pater or Ruskin; as this picture or rather evocation of Greek art in its golden age:

The sculptor hewed from the marble block the great white-limbed Hermes that slept within it. The waxers and gilders of images gave tone and texture to the statue, and the world, when it saw it, worshipped and was dumb. * * * From the river valley he took the fine clay in his fingers and with a little tool of wood or bone, fashioned it into forms so exquisite that people gave them to the dead as their playthings, and we find them still in the dusty tombs on the yellow hillside by Tanagra, with the faint gold and the fading crimson still lingering about hair and lips and raiment. On a wall of fresh plaster, stained with bright sandyx, he pictured one who trod with tired feet the purple, white-starred fields of asphodel, one "in whose eyelids lay the whole of the Trojan War." * * * He held the gem against the revolving disk, and the amethyst became the purple couch of Adonis, and across the veined sardonyx sped Artemis with her hounds. He beat out the gold into roses, and strung them together for necklace or armlet. He beat out the gold for wreaths for the conqueror's helmet, or into palmates for the Tyrian robe or into masks for the royal dead. On the back of the silver mirror he graved Thetis borne by her Nereids, or love-sick Phœdra with her nurse, or Persephone, weary of memory, putting poppies in her hair. The potter sat in his shed, and flower-like from the silent wheel, the vase rose up beneath his hands.

## V

It is remarkable how much Wilde seems to lean upon books and the cultural tradition in his writings. He gives us all too lavishly of his reading, and yet he had touched life at many points, and was to know the extremes of fortune. He shrank from unpleasant realities, as we know, with a perverse aloofness that was part of his pose, maybe, but that was also part of his nature. In his prosperous times he refused to look upon and shunned contact with ugly or unfortunate people, though his charity and kind-heartedness are well attested. After his prison experiences he hated to talk about them, still less to make "copy" of them, refusing very liberal offers from French and American newspapers, although he was in keen stress for money at the time. *De Profundis,* which glances at his life in prison, was not published until after his death; and while the *Ballad of Reading Gaol,* given to the world with his cell number, and universally known as his work, may seem to mark an inconsistency, it was not so in fact, at least to his mind, in view of the intended symbolical character of the poem.

Here we touch upon a vital trait of Wilde, one that coloured both his life and art; also maybe it suggests a strong reason for his enduring popularity. I have already pointed out his marked instinct and talent for success, amounting well-nigh to genius. Certain it is that the world likes a cheerful tale and lends a reluctant ear to the "hard-luck story," shunning the contagion of poverty and misfortune. American magazines have capitalized this vulgar optimism, and not a few men have escaped the failure which mediocre abilities seemed to guarantee them by a persistent preaching up of success in the material aims of life. Not an exalted philosophy, in any view of it, founded as it is upon a shrewd regard to the main chance. There can be no question, at any rate, that it served (and still serves) Wilde well in his fantastic yet intelligently conceived use of it. He censured the stern realism of Maupassant, tearing the rags from and exposing the sores of human nature. In his view, art should be a medium for presenting only agreeable and lovely things—nothing else merited a place in the record. He shrank with no affected shudder from all that was wretched and repulsive—the foul odors of poverty, the unlovely dialect of the poor, the gross manners of those outside the charmed circle of caste * —all contacts disagreeable to the "best society." He is never done pointing his gibes at the middle class, to which he in fact belonged, as his "friend," Lord Alfred Douglas, is at pains to inform us. He wanted to write for and about people of social position,—an ideal perfectly realized in his plays, which are "plush" in the superlative degree; to brand their moral peccadilloes with a light hand, proving that beyond measure he admired and envied even while he satirized them. He played for them, he talked for them, he lived for them, and without them he could not imagine a tolerable world. That he was a snob, at least in the Thackeravian degree

* Wilde never gave us a truer line on himself than when he said that it was a bore to be in society but hell to be on the outside!

of confession, cannot be denied; he would not have rejected the name for himself, but he would have insisted upon defining it in his own terms.

Artistically there is nothing to reprehend in all this, and the attitude was most fortunate for Wilde, as it insured the success of his plays, "Lady Windermere's Fan," "An Ideal Husband," etc., which are justly held to be the finest examples of artificial comedy that the stage has known since the day of Sheridan. It is not pretended that Wilde brought new matter to the drama, or that he "profoundly influenced the art of the theatre," as the phrase goes, or even that he excels in novelty of situation and ingenuity of plot. His social comedies offer little more than a clever apportionment of glittering dialogue among some specious marionettes,* but they never fail to interest, in spite of the admitted tenuity of the dramatic motive. The copy of upper-class manners is held to be sufficiently authentic, the wit is more refined than Sheridan's and the paradox utterly beyond him; moreover (not to

*Lady Windermere's Fan* is something more and better, of course; there can be no question that Wilde was on his way to finer achievement in the drama when his disaster befell.

drop our *leitmotif)* the charm is always the Wildean charm which goes *sans* definition. Of these dramatic diversions the lightest and happiest is the *Importance of Being Earnest;* it may well be called the comedy of golden, careless youth—well-bred English youth, of course, delightfully snobbish and engaging, also wittier than is the privilege of correct society. This piece enthroned Wilde as lord of the lighter theatre, and it marks the highest point of fame and success which he had scored before his downfall.

## VI

It is as the author of so-called "society plays," brilliant, superficial, factitious, and disdainfully conventional, that Wilde has most fortunately struck the public imagination, and perhaps the rehabilitation of his fame is in great part to be ascribed to these works.* A play does far more for reputation

* Bernard Shaw's success is so emphatically due to an aggressive personality that one hardly thinks of the share Fate has had in it. But it is certain that Shaw did not begin to come into his own until Wilde's disgrace had removed the more attractive, if not more highly gifted, Irishman from the scene. In a very real way the downfall of Wilde made room and opportunity for Shaw.

than a book—Wilde, the mere poet and essayist, might never have won back to the light of day. The social *câchet* is upon these dramatic *divertissements* (supra-clever, if not masterpieces), and so they continue to fillip the indifferent wits of the "smart set," or to amuse correct and respectable people who would regard the *Ballad of Reading Gaol* as an aberration, and who could not be moved to turn a page of the *Soul of Man Under Socialism.*

Perhaps the two works of Wilde which have made his name most widely known are *The Picture of Dorian Gray* and *Salome;* the one a kind of psychological *quasi*-novel, the other what must, I suppose, be called a poetical tragedy. In spite of the great celebrity they have attained, these productions are of slight originality and, in a critical view, scarcely justify the noise they have made in the world. For the morbid conception of the novel Wilde sat to Stevenson and others, though one must allow that his literary handling of the borrowed conception offers not a little of his most powerful pen-work. In spite of whatever disparagement, "Dorian Gray" stands in the first rank of Wilde's books by reason of its meticulously wrought style, which yet produces an effect of brilliant carelessness, and its intense personality. Doubtless the chief reason for the great and continuing vogue of this book is that the public persists in identifying Wilde with the hero of his sinister yet magnetic fable, and reading therein his secret biography—by way of introduction to "De Profundis," as one might say without flippancy.

"Salome" was lifted and "adapted" from Flaubert (without acknowledgment) and is altogether a slighter, inferior piece of work, though of the first order in point of audacity and morbid fascination. Wilde connoisseurs prize it for the Sadistic suggestion that permeates it and find therein curious points of comparison with his darker personal legend. It is the most perverse of Wilde's performances, the farthest fling of his lawless fancy; and in plain language, it has much to shock the scrupulous reader. Also, to be fair, it is not without a strange and malign beauty; in especial the artist in words, the jeweller of speech, exerts himself with a quite diabolical skill to ensnare and captivate us. Yes, there is much to admire in "Salome," despite its dénouement unwarranted in history or legend, despite its eroto-haemotological offensiveness. After the reader has had his "thrill" with it, I would advise that he take up "Herodias" by Gustave Flaubert, a literary masterpiece and a marvellous feat of historical evocation. Therein he will find that he owes something of apology to the guilty yet too much slandered daughter of the Tetrarch's queen.

I would not close this too cursive notice of the man and his work without adding a word upon that most interesting fragrant, "A Florentine Tragedy." Here is the thing that Wilde could have done better than any of his rivals and that one likes to think he was on the way to doing in its fulness when his career was so suddenly blighted. I doubt if the native genius of Wilde,—the unborrowed, unassimilated essence of his talent,—appears anywhere to so marked advantage as in this poetical torso. It remains in its unfinished state * a striking memorial of the, alas, too famous and unfortunate author.

* In some recent editions a substitute for the missing first act is supplied by Mr. Sturge Moore—with a high degree of success, it must be allowed. One hardly agrees with the view that Wilde, always perverse, finished the tail of the piece first and never returned to the head:—in point of fact he several times refers

Finally, with the approval of all who love letters, the lucky star of Oscar Wilde is again in the ascendant, with the complete retrieval of his fame and the saving of his literary achievement unto future times.

to it as if it were completed work. More likely the missing part was stolen amid the general looting and dispersion of his effects that followed his conviction; but why it has not since been offered in the market baffles conjecture.

## A CENSOR OF RENAN

### I

THE study of Renan in Frank Harris's "Contemporary Portraits," while one of the most pretentious in the book, and strongly written in parts—the fine passionate outburst on Paul, for example—to my mind often verges on caricature. This essay also displays a curious sort of courage in Mr. Harris, an overweening self-assertion toward his more or less eminent subjects or "sitters," which it is seldom easy to take at his own valuation. He sometimes gives himself the upper-hand of Renan in their alleged debates—not an unusual proceeding of Mr. Harris in dealing with his subjects, by the bye. Renan did not speak English, and his interviewer fails to mention how these copious dialogues were conducted. One can hardly suppose that it was in French?—but this is perhaps too delicate a question! At any rate, Mr. Harris allots himself the best speeches, deals himself the choice trumps, as it were, in these séances with the author of the "Vie de Jésus"—he, the relatively obscure journalist, who should have been thrilled to his marrow with the pride of listening to the greatest liberal scholar, the most eloquent talker in Europe. And of his own talk, which he reports with no excess of modesty, he says: "He (Renan) swallowed it all greedily, smiling and twirling his thumbs. . . . But it was not worth while to try to correct his illimitable conceit."

This is sufficiently arresting, even from one who is "always artist rather than reporter" and who pretends to "spiritual divination and not to verbal accuracy." * Whatever the apocryphal note of these discourses, their imaginative daring, not to say impudence, will easily be conceded.

Mr. Harris is at pains to make M. Renan (and the reader) listen to his strictures upon the "Life of Jesus," which are not remarkable for point or profundity; and he pictures Renan as eager to hear and contest them, although his book had years before been attacked from every standpoint by the ablest Christian apologists in Europe. "Renan's longing

* Vide Preface to Mr. Harris's "My Contemporaries."

for praise seemed to me almost childish," says our judicious author. "What can praise or blame matter to one who knows he has done his work? His cawing like a hungry baby-rook for a morsel of praise stiffened me." . . . Mr. Harris is perhaps nowhere else in his book so amusing as in this paper on Renan. And surely nowhere else does his rôle of artistic reporter seem to bear so severe a strain.

However, there is a worse thing than his "patronizing" of Renan, and that is his caricaturing of him. I do not recall ever having read so gross a libel and travesty upon a man whose life and writings were known to all the world. Mr. Harris denies the virtue of truth to the great man who chose the words *Veritatem dilexi* (I have loved the truth) for his tombstone. He then proceeds to more painful and unwarranted censure:

"Again and again one is brought up with a shock by his (Renan's) extraordinary, abnormal sensuality. Here are really the two poles between which the man swings. He was a hopeless unbeliever, and at the same time given over to all pleasures, —pleasures of thought, pleasures of sentiment (his heroes love to weep like women), pleasures of the senses. As we have seen, he was gross in body, indolent physically; altogether unable to appreciate finely either an athlete or a saint, much less a hero."

Again: "He (Renan) takes himself for a measure of the Ideal, and he is not justified. The reason of his failure is unmistakable. First of all, he is a Frenchman, and the French are somewhat obsessed by the sense of sex, apt to be too much given to sensual delights. Then, too, Renan was brought up as a priest and his natural desires thereby subjected to unnatural restraint. In consequence of this he seems to have found sex-attraction quite irresistible; he is weaker even than the ordinary Frenchman: he does not only yield to temptation; he seeks it out."

All this seems to me assertion without proof, slander lightly carried on the facile journalistic word, and I am sure it will not be acquiesced in by those who know their Renan. It is ridiculous of Mr. Harris to take the play of "L'Abbesse de Jouarre" as proving the case against Renan. Even Father Barry, in his life of Renan, anxious as a Roman Catholic priest should be to discredit and diminish the great infidel whom other priests did not scruple to call the Anti-Christ, does not go so far. He censures the work indeed (an intellectual diversion of the author's old age), but he does not pretend to find in it a sure ground for postulating Renan's personal immorality. The worst that Dr. Barry can bring himself to say is this:

"Himself a rare example of hard work, sober, studious, moderate, decorous, whose life hid nothing of which he need be ashamed, he followed after the multitude, not to sin as they did, but in flowery phrases to condone their sinning."

Here Father Barry, a stern theologian of the faith which Renan abandoned, reads a lesson in charity to Frank Harris, a writer who has never been accused of slurring the sex-motive in his various productions. The true explanation is that Father Barry was better informed than Mr. Harris as to the literary works, the hermeneutic labors, and the moral character of Renan, and he was far better qualified to judge him, both as a man and as a master of Biblical exegesis. Also he was without the vices of "snap" judgment and hasty writing, which unfortunately sometimes pertain to the "artist as reporter." Furthermore, the dashing semi-imaginative or apocryphal interview methods used by Mr. Frank Harris, would not have commended themselves to the strictly veracious biographer of Renan.

## II

I have been reading Renan for thirty years and still count the "Souvenirs de Ma Jeunesse" as marking an epoch in my intellectual growth. (It is one of the books I reread at least every other year.) I believe one can admire him prodigiously without believing that he destroyed the Christ of Revelation, and that one may dislike the freedom of certain writings of his (I do not myself) without therein finding reason to impeach the purity of his life. Now having been a student of Renan all those years, and having overlooked nothing of real credit and importance that has been written about him in French or English, I do not hesitate to say that Mr. Harris will do well to expunge this offensive matter from future editions of his book, if such shall be called for. It is bad criticism besides, marking an awkward inconsistency in the author, some of whose essays in fiction claim a large tolerance on moral grounds. Also I recommend him to correct throughout this essay the superior tone which he maintains toward his distinguished subject (not, as I have pointed out, a solitary instance):—it is truly of a sort to make the judicious grieve!

Renan's own view of his personal morality and his sense of responsibility in this regard, is set down in the "Souvenirs," above referred to, one of the last and most delightful works of his pen, which he clearly intended as an *apologia* for his whole life. The candor and complete honesty of the following statement have never been questioned by the fair-minded:

"My clerical ideas have exercised a still greater influence over me in all that relates to the rules of morality. I should have looked upon it as a lack of decorum if I had made any change in my habits upon this score. The world at large, in its ignorance of spiritual things, believes that men only abandon the ecclesiastical calling because they find its duties too severe. I should never have forgiven myself if I had done anything to lend even a semblance of reason to views so superficial. With my extreme conscientiousness, I was anxious to be at peace with myself, and I continued to live in Paris the life which I had led in the Seminary. . . . Thus it may upon the whole be said, that I have come short in little of my clerical promises. I have exchanged spirituality for ideality. I have been truer to my engagements than many priests apparently more regular in their conduct."

To conclude: the rich intellectuality of Renan on a few occasions led him to express himself with a measure of the Latin freedom of thought and the license granted to French writers: upon so much and no more rest Mr. Harris's strictures. One recalls that Renan was too priest-like, too deprecatory and debonair for the forthright, uncompromising Ingersoll. Of the Frenchman he shrewdly said: "He left the Church, but he carried the incense of the altar a long way with him."

ERNEST RENAN

# THE LESBIAN

## I

O my youth, my youth, who has you now?
I shall never know you again!

THIS is a fragment of Sappho the peerless and, as it seems to me, one of the loveliest, most touching and memorable cries of song. Alas that we should have of her scarcely more than a cry!

The anthology of literature has nothing to rival the so slight yet ineffably precious remains of Sappho. These are scarcely more than echoes of her matchless singing,—a line or two, a broken stanza, a thought just leaving the Poet like a bird from her hand—but the charm, the fragrance, the mystery of a unique personality hang ineffaceably about them. The broken vase forever haunted with the scent of the roses it once contained—this is the relique of literature we name Sappho.

Yet unspeakably slight though it be, somehow it suffices to convey her essence, her supreme, heart-searching quality. I doubt if the Annals of Poesy may offer a more precious gift, a more hallowed fame. The persistence of that lovely voice, while so many centuries have been entombed and the Isles of Greece have so strangely altered their destinies, seems to me as thrilling a thought as literature is capable of inspiring. It is Greece herself, that vision of intellectual glory and perfect beauty, whom we adore in these relics of her supreme woman Poet!

Curiosity eternally pursues "burning Sappho" even as it does Helen, that other wondrous type of the Greek genius: each is supreme in her fashion; the one by her beauty, the other by her song. And marvelous to relate, after so many ages gone to dust the world is still haunted by desire of them both, as of a sweetness that can never be tasted unto cloying.

So the poets, ever enamored of the violet-crowned Lesbian, continue to seek from her the secret of her imperishable charm. They turn and re-turn her lovely words in a despair of conveying that essence which has defied the rasure of time. Sometimes they achieve at least a hint of her divine grace and perfection, as in these renderings by Edward Storer, a contemporary English poet.

How many restless thoughts recall to me
The sterile Atthis, and I long for the slender one.
Sadness devours my soul. From far there comes
to us
The sound of her sharp cry, and it is not
Unheard, for Night, the many-eared, carries it
To us across the sea that flows between.

* * *

The moon has set and the Pleiades
Have gone.
It is midnight; the hours pass; and I sleep alone.

* * *

Love shakes my soul.
So do the oak-trees on the mountain
Shake in the wind.

* * *

I have a lovely child, like a flower of gold, Kleis,
Whom I would not sell for the wealth of all
Lydia.

* * *

As the apple ripening on the bough, the furthermost
Bough of all the tree, is never noticed by the gatherers,
Or, being out of reach, is never plucked at all.

* * *

The stars of night gathered round the moon will veil their bright
Faces when she grows full and lights everything with silver.

* * *

Night, you who gather in your lovely lap
The things the shining dawn flung far and wide,
The ewe-lamb you bring back, the straying goat,
The child unto its mother's side.

## II

There dwells amongst us a pure Pelasgian, by name John Myers O'Hara, who has made good his Hellenic descent by publishing a translation of Sappho, the first of all poets of passion.

How much Aeolic went into the making of this version of Sappho I know not, and indeed the point is of small importance; what we have to be thankful for is a rendering of the deathless Muse of Mitylene, in several respects the most admirable and complete that has yet been achieved in English.

Mr. O'Hara's version is synthetic as well as interpretative—that is to say, he is equal parts poet and translator, the rarest of equations. From the four hundred odd lines which are all that remain of "burning Sappho"—the rest having perished, according to accepted tradition, at the hands of the monks, jealous of the poetical fame of St. Gregory Naziensen—he has built up a series of poems each complete in itself; gems from Sappho's girdle, if not wholly brilliants from her diadem.

Most of the poems are unrhymed, thus preserving the Greek *vraisemblance*, and not a few of them are in the difficult Sapphic metre: yet they are flowing and musical, most cunningly assonant and happily phrased beyond any like translations known to me. Take, for example, these lines from the famous, often translated and imitated but never equaled fragment, the immortal hymn of passion which Mr. O'Hara has expanded into his *Ode to Anactoria.*

Peer of gods to me is the man thy presence
Crowns with joy; who hears as he sits beside thee
Accents sweet of thy lips the silence breaking
With lovely laughter;

Tones that make the heart in my bosom flutter,
For if I, the space of a moment even,
Near to thee come, any words I would utter
Instantly fail me.

Vain my stricken tongue would a whisper fashion,
Subtly under my skin runs fire ecstatic;
Straightway mists surge dim to my eyes and leave
them
Reft of their vision.

Echoes ring in my ears; a trembling seizes
All my body bathed in soft perspiration;
Pale as grass I grow in my passion's madness,
Like one insensate.

How this divine Song of Love escaped the monks, when so much else that was Sappho's perished for the good of men's souls, remains a marvel. No doubt there is a Providence in Art as in religion. And certain it is that those blind and stupid attempts to put out the lovely fire Sappho kindled in the hearts of men have caused her fame to be justly rated among the most unique and precious things in the keeping of the world. Immortal and scatheless, she smiles upon us at a distance of twenty-five centuries. And be it remarked, the poems of St. Gregory Nazienzen are no longer read, even by the monks themselves. Thus is the Devil sometimes permitted to work his malice in this world.

It is a far cry from olive-crowned, sweetly smiling Mytilene, queen of the Lesbian isle, in the fifth or sixth century B. C., to the present graceless Epoch. Yet in these versions of Mr. O'Hara the Spirit of Poetry has achieved an unlooked-for miracle. The most passionate soul that ever breathed her longings to the lyre, the loveliest and most memorable spirit of antiquity, here speaks to us in authentic accents and in terms of ecstasy only possible to herself and her fair white gods.

Reading these poems, which are at once a litany of passion and a perfection of Art, one is involuntarily seized by the old pagan madness for youth and beauty and sin that knew itself not as sin—by a desire almost nympholeptic for that vanished world which held so much that is denied to us, redeemed—and at the same time hopelessly depoetized by our Christian faith.

This pure Greek by name O'Hara is the most fortunate of translators, because he is himself a lover and a poet. Sappho, dreaming of Phaon, has kissed him on the lips and over the heart, and then with a divine gesture tossed him some leaves from her garland. To him, as to the great English singer, has it been given to see—

> "the white implacable Aphrodite,
> See the hair unbound and the feet unsandaled
> Shine as fire of sunset on western waters;
> See the reluctant
> "Feet, the straining plumes of the doves that drew her,
> Looking always, with their necks reverted
> Back to Lesbos—back to the hills whereunder
> Shone Mitylene."

Many writers have labored to express their appreciation of these fragments—strayed notes from the Lesbian's lyre; and still more numerous are they who have vainly sought to imitate their strange longing, their mixture of the earthly and the celes-

"MUSE IMMORTAL, SAPPHO!"
An ancient bust in the Vatican, Rome

tial. The lines to Anactoria depicting the ecstasy of love's desire and never approached by even the greatest poets—the apple on the highest bough—the image of ingathering Night,—these are among the eternal crown jewels of Poetry. But who would be so absurd as to venture a commentary on Sappho—that is to say, on Perfection! Let us rather humbly give thanks that we may taste and enjoy her immortal beauty. She is herself the Apple on the highest bough of Poesy!

Long before she fell foul of St. Gregory and the monks Sappho was the mark for a peculiar species of sexual slander which still attaints her fame, though it must be allowed, on no very tangible grounds. Alas, this mephitic sort of glory has never failed her—from Daudet in our time back to Horace even great literary men have pursued the Lesbian, jealous no doubt of her secure immortality. I mention Horace (whose own confessions, by the bye, put him out of court) because he has a few celebrated lines which have been too freely rendered, to Sappho's discredit, associating her glorious name with a *culpa infanda:*

Quam paene furvae regna Proserpinae
Et judicantem vidimus Aeacum
Sedesque discretas piorum et
Aeoliis fidibus querentem
Sappho puellis de popularibus!

Which may be paraphrased:

Almost we chanced upon the awful sight
Of Aeacus judging in the realm below
Of gloomy shades, where sable rivers flow;
Almost we glimpsed th' abode of spirits bright,
And Sappho heard fretting upon her lyre
A plaint of fickle maids that had forgot her fire.

There are some harshly judging persons who see in the tragic fate of Sappho, following her lover Phaon to a watery grave,* and in the age-long persistence of the scandals pursuing her memory, a salient instance of the avenging hand of Nemesis. We remain ourselves firmly persuaded that she has not been convicted of any worse offence than that of writing the finest poems of human passion this world has ever known.

* Another legend, less romantic but more likely, has it that she survived to a good old age.

# A FRIEND OF LAFCADIO HEARN

AMONG the few Americans who perished as a result of the recent earthquake * in Japan, the most notable was Capt. Mitchell McDonald, famous in literary circles the world over for his friendship with Lafcadio Hearn. It is not so well known that since the writer's death and up to the last hour of his own life McDonald exercised a benevolent guardianship over Hearn's family and very capably managed his literary estate. There are few instances known to me of a mere "layman" taking up such a trust—I refer to the literary executorship—late in life and acquitting himself thereof with such eminent credit. The net result of McDonald's efforts was greatly to extend the literary fame of his friend and to make a solid provision for his family. Hearn, it will be recalled, married a Japanese woman who survives with four children. Capt. McDonald's will, it is understood,

* Fall of 1923.

continues the generous measure of support which the family have heretofore received from him.

Capt. McDonald served for many years in the United States Navy as Paymaster, which office carries the courtesy title of Captain. While still in the service he became the principal owner of the Grand Hotel at Yokohama—one of the best known hotels in the East—which was utterly destroyed by the earthquake. It was here that his friendship with Lafcadio Hearn began, about 1905, and most of the meetings referred to below took place at the hotel. Lafcadio was as shy as a bird, and his fear of meeting strangers amounted to an obsession of almost comic intensity. That he lent himself so often to Capt. McDonald's hospitable intentions, is the strongest possible testimony to the genial warmheartedness of his friend.

Mitchell McDonald was indeed a man of whom it might be said that he had a genius for friendship. Paradoxically enough, though known to so many the world over and loved as few men are, modesty was, next to generosity, his most remarkable trait. Simple, frank, soldierly, of the warmest affections and the most scrupulous loyalty, he was such a man as is rarely met with, outside the pages of romance; and to fully realize him one should imagine a character resulting from a collaboration of Lever and Dumas.

All this would seem to justify the publication of some notes which I made after my first meeting with Capt. McDonald many years ago, at the Bellevue-Stratford hotel in Philadelphia. I offer them without change or re-editing.

Being a little ahead of the appointed time, I gave myself up to the pleasure of anticipating the long planned-for meeting. It did not occur to me that I should fail to recognize McDonald by any chance, though I had never seen him in the flesh. The fact was, I had often studied an excellent portrait of him in a favorite book of mine, the "Life and Letters of Lafcadio Hearn." Also I had given some attention to the moral likeness of him afforded by the same interesting work, which had given me a strong desire to know the man.

And so I went about the Bellevue lobbies and corridors, looking for a broad-shouldered, brown-haired, bright-eyed man in his middle thirties, wearing the uniform of an American naval officer. With such a picture of him in my mind's eye, and seeing moreover that he likewise would be looking for me, it seemed a reasonable certainty that I could not miss him.

But I did, however, having forgotten to allow for a little matter of a dozen years or so; and he hailed me first. The broad shoulders were the same, but wearing a civilian dress-coat; the brown hair was mixed with gray; the full moustache was nearly white; and the eyes were still bright, only they now twinkled behind glasses. I thought, with a whimsical momentary disappointment, of the dashing young officer whom Lafcadio Hearn had loved and trusted beyond any of the few whom he took into the inner circle of his friendship:—and then I felt the eloquent grip of Mitchell McDonald. After this first impression the Captain grew younger every minute, and ere the evening ended (somewhat toward the morning) I had fully rediscovered the man of the portrait. . . .

A friend of Lafcadio Hearn! Not so long ago the bitter memories of certain haters of Hearn gave these words an ironical meaning. But the haters have had their say and are now silent: a wiser and kinder judgment begins to prevail.

Yet it may freely be granted that if ever there lived a man with whom it was difficult to maintain an equable friendship, that man was Lafcadio Hearn. His hair-trigger susceptibility to offence, his appalling frankness toward friend and foe alike, his tarantula-like readiness to strike, his exacting though just conception of what was due himself, his touchy independence, his hatred of merely conventional amenities, and, above all, a morbid distrust confirmed by many years of experience only too bitter, conspired to render his friendship a perilous, if inestimable gift. In nothing was he more *difficile* than in his terrible candor—the exercise of this quality cost him some friends who stood silent when they should have defended his grave.

But that Hearn, with all his varied "impossibility," was capable of both feeling and inspiring a genuine and worthy friendship, his relations with Capt. McDonald abundantly prove. The page is one of the most cheerful in a life that never was over-bright and that had known too few such pages;

the letters which it called forth from Hearn are among the best and wholesomest and most humanly interesting that he has left us. This is saying much, for better letters than those of Lafcadio Hearn have not been written since Charles Lamb died, leaving the very best letters in the world.

I beg to subjoin a few extracts from Hearn's correspondence with Mitchell McDonald which do full justice to their friendship, and now that the record is closed forever, reflect equal honor upon both.

In January, 1898, Hearn writes from Tokyo to Capt. McDonald in Yokohama where the latter was attached as Paymaster to the U. S. Naval Hospital:

I believe those days of mine in Yokohama were the most pleasurable in a pilgrimage of forty-seven years. Such experience will not do for me, except at vast intervals. It sends me back to work with much too good an opinion of myself—and that is bad for literary self-judgment. The beneficial result is an offsetting of that morbid condition—that utter want of self-confidence. * * * I not only feel that I ought to do something good, but I am going to do it,—with the permission of the gods.

The characteristic shyness of the man, which made him shun anything of the nature of "social functions," appears in this extract:

How to answer your kind suggestion about pulling me out of my shell, I don't well know. I like to be out of the shell—but much of that kind of thing could only result in the blue devils. After seeing men like you and the other Guardsman,—the dear Doctor,—one is beset with a foolish wish to get back into the world which produced you both.

Again the note of self-distrust—Hearn seems never to have foreseen the sudden fulness of fame and literary appreciation that followed close upon his death:

It would do me a great deal of harm if I could believe your appreciations and predictions, but I am quite sure you are mistaken about both. * * * You are making me talk too much about my own affairs, and you would really spoil me if you could. * * * About the truth of life seems to be this: You can get what you wish only when you have stopped wishing for it and do not care about keeping it.

The next selection has reference to an investment proposition which Capt. McDonald (a good man of business) had brought to his notice. Hearn's dread of business was comic in its intensity. This excerpt reveals the humorist, of whom we have too little in Hearn's formal work:

I read the prospectus with great interest * * * And I am proud of my friend. "Canst thou play with Leviathan like a bird? Or canst thou bind him for thy handmaidens?" No, I can't, and I am not going to try, but I have a friend in Yokohama—an officer of the U. S. Navy—*he* plays with Leviathan and makes him "talk soft, soft words" —indeed he even "presses down his tongue with a cord." * * * But as for *me*—the greatest favor you can ever do me is to take off my hands even the business I have,—contracts and the like,—so that I need never again remember them. Besides, if I were dead, you are the one I should want to be profiting by my labors. Then every time you set your jaw square and made them "fork over," my ghost would squeak and chipper for delight,—and you would look around to see where the bats came from!

The shortest letter in the entire collection, but one that throws a strong light on both Hearn and his friend, is this, dated March, 1898:

I do not feel pleased at your returning to me the money and giving me your own copy of the book. I feel mean over it. But what can one do with a man who deliberately takes off his own coat to cover his friend during a nine-minutes' drive? I shall remember the *feeling* of that coat until I die.

The sensitiveness and worldly wisdom—for he had the artist's wisdom and sagacity of observation, if not in action—are sharply evident in this extract:

My Boston friend is lost to me, certainly. I got a letter yesterday from him—showing the serious effect upon friendship of taking to one's self a wife, —a fashionable wife. It was meant to be exactly like the old letters;—but it wasn't. Paymaster M. M. must also some day take a wife, and . . . oh! I know what you are going to say,—they all say *that!* They all assure you that they *both* love you, and that their house will always be open to you, etc., etc., and then they forget all about you—purposely or otherwise. Still, one ought to be grateful,—the dropping is so gentle, and softly done!

The following is remarkable for its literary interest, disclosing the eternal expectation of the artist, as well as the confidence which Hearn thus early (1898) manifests in the man who was destined to become his literary executor:

In case that during this year, or any year, there should come to me a good idea for such a story as I have been long hoping to write * * * then I shall abandon everything else for the time being and write it. If I can ever write *that,* there will be money in it, long after I have been planted in one of these old Buddhist cemeteries * * * What divine luck such an inspiration would be! But the chances are that a more powerful mind than mine will catch the inspiration first,—as the highest peak most quickly takes the sun. Whatever comes, I'll just hand or send the MS. to you, and say, "Now just do whatever you please—only see that I get the proofs. The book is yours."

And here is a rare view of the devoted literary artist who, his work being in question, scorned to mince ceremony even with his dearest friend:

I am going to ask you simply *not* to come and see your friend, and *not* to ask him to come to see you, *for at least three months more.* I know this seems horrid—but such are the conditions upon which literary work alone is possible, when combined with the duties of a professor of literature. I don't want to see or hear or feel anything outside of my work until the book is done,—and I therefore have the impudent assurance to ask you to help me stand by my wheel.

Capable of friendship and kindness surely was the man who wrote this to his friend:

Do you know that we talked uninterruptedly the other day for ten hours,—for the period that people are wont to qualify when speaking of the enormity of time as *"ten mortal hours?"* What a pity they could not be made immortal! They always will be with me.

Or this, with which I must conclude the delightful but too seductive task of making these extracts,—conclude with regret, for I have scarcely uncovered the riches of the vein:

I suppose you have heard of the famous old drama which has for its title, "The Woman Killed with Kindness." Presently, if you do not take care, you will be furnishing the material for a much more modern tragedy, to be called "The Small Man Killed with Kindness." * * * That whiskey! Those cigars! That wonderful beefsteak! Those imperial and sinfully splendid dinners! Those wonderful chats until ghost-time and beyond it! And all those things—however pleasing in themselves—made like a happy dream by multitudes of little acts and words and thoughts that created about me an atmosphere not belonging at all to this world of Iron Facts and Granite Necessities.

It is good to know that Hearn's confidence in his friend has been more than justified. When Dr. Gould published his crude and vindictive disparagement of Hearn, he found in Captain McDonald a champion who was neither to be poohpoohed into silence nor cajoled into complaisance. In a word, the misguided Gould discovered that he had a fighter on his hands who seemed to like the game the better, the harder it was made for him (McDonald was Pennsylvania Irish, a rather wicked fighting strain). Together with Ellwood Hendrick, another stanch friend of Hearn, he soon forced Gould to battle for his life. The latter's book or rather libel on Hearn,—perhaps the coldest-blooded and most deliberate attempt ever made to degrade a man of true genius,—fell dead on the market after having been repudiated and condemned by all honest critics both at home and abroad.

Finally, the estate, literary and other, has been so wisely managed that it is now adequate to support the writer's family (living in Japan) in considerable comfort. McDonald has obtained prices for Hearn's work that truly would have made the latter "squeak and chipper." Also by retrieving and publishing Hearn's Japanese lectures McDonald has richly added to the literary bequest of his friend. The fame of Hearn is both rising and spreading; the best of his books have been translated into the principal European languages; he seems thus soon to be ranked among the world's classics.

In all that has now been written there was nothing to qualify my pleasure at meeting Captain McDonald, and certainly nothing to prevent our having a good dinner with the Captain as host—a part for which he was born, not made. That our talk ran almost wholly upon Hearn, goes without saying. One thing only I may set down as showing the loyalty and loveliness of the friendship between these men, so dissimilar in most external respects. Mention being made of certain caricatures of Hearn's physical appearance put forth in ignorance or hatred or envy, the Captain said simply: "He seemed always beautiful to me!" . . .

Ah, Koizumi! * if perchance your honorable spirit hovered about us in the Bellevue that night, —in the city where once you tarried poor, unknown and with but scant hope until Destiny called you to the Far East and the making of a deathless name,— sure am I that you saw and heard only what deepened your love for your friend.

* Yakumo Koizumi, name adopted by Hearn upon his marriage.

## ELBERT HUBBARD

ELBERT HUBBARD was a fatalist. I saw this from an early moment of our acquaintance. Those solemn words of the Preacher —*The race is not to the swift nor the battle to the strong,*—were often on his lips and frequently cropped up in his writings, as if they were the ground-note of his thought. From the same text he chose the words "Time and Chance" as a title for his novelized life of John Brown of Osawatomie—a book which throws a more interesting light on Elbert Hubbard than on John Brown. I think they were never far absent from his thought, and they were the first to leap into my mind on the earliest rumor of his fate. For here indeed was a case, if ever there were one, in which the race was not to the swift nor the battle to the strong!

I have said that he was a fatalist. Many took this trait for a pose; some deduced from it a character for heartlessness, which they freely thrust upon him. Both were wrong. His fatalism was deeply rooted in his nature, and it imparted a certain melancholy Hamlet-like charm to his personality (I speak of him as I first knew him). His gait was that of a man who would be wise and cautious in all ways, but who knew that the ordering of ultimate destinies is not within any man's power. He carried himself bravely and jauntily, yet with circumspection; and often he seemed to pause and listen for a word of the Fates. I could not imagine him playing the coward to Destiny. Short as was the grace allowed him, I believe he stood up like a brave man in the last awful moment, and that no man on the *Lusitania* met his death with a stronger soul.*

That Elbert Hubbard was a many-sided man is shown by our anxiety to analyze him. He was hateful to some, beloved by many, interesting to all, indifferent to few.

There was a mystic in Elbert Hubbard, suppressed or subordinated in those later years when responding to the conditions of his public fame, he

* Elbert Hubbard and his wife Alice were among the many lost with the *Lusitania,* torpedoed off the Irish coast May, 1915. This paper is in substance an address given by the Author at the Memorial Convention held at East Aurora, July 4–11, 1915.

lived his life too much on the outside and aimed consciously to hold the crowd. This mystical note was strong in the man on his first appearance as a writer, and I think for his better audience it has always been the heart of his appeal. He had been an early and profound reader of the Bible, and there was a time—a few years before he started the "Philistine"—when he had thoughts of entering the ministry. On our first meeting not long afterward, I noticed a something about him that smacked of the country parson. His speech had a biblical accent and his writings were strongly marked with the same *—indeed he once told me that the Bible and Emerson were the only books he had ever read *for the love of them.* He belonged at this time to the Universalist communion and he quietly but effectively led his visitors to church—as in later years he shepherded them to the Roycroft Chapel.

* See especially the Essays, "Why I am a Philistine," "The Song of Songs," the "Book of Job," "The Book of Ecclesiastes" in the book entitled "As it Seems to Me"—all strong and characteristic work which belongs to his earlier and, as one may say, more *literary* period. I mean only that in those years, the infancy of the Roycroft, he thought more of writing for its own sake and gave more of himself to this dearest of his ambitions.

This suggestion of the mystic went well with his subdued voice, his gentle manners, his shy yet potent personality (again I speak of the man of twenty years ago). It made, I believe, a great part of his fascination for women, and no man of our time has fascinated women more, ascetic as he was at heart; but this too, no doubt, had its lure. Best of all, this hint of the mystic gave a charm to his earlier writings which, as I have said, is too much lacking in his later work. The growth of the Roycroft somewhat spoiled the dreamer, and success itself cheapened or profaned the "heart of his mystery."

Many a devotee has wavered between marriage and the convent. Some famous heretics have long hesitated between faith and skepticism, and nearly all of them have begun as firm believers. I wonder if Elbert Hubbard, whom at thirty-five a straw would have decided for the ministry, was not led by blind forces farther than he wished at heart to go. Surely the hard agnosticism of his later period, and the flippant rejection of man's loftiest hope—which I have always felt to be out of character with the true Elbert Hubbard—were a poor exchange for the old-time gentle mysticism and the dream that often recalled his master Emerson.

The dogmatist of infidelity is apt to become as intolerant as the dogmatist of revealed religion. This was the vice of Ingersoll—the fury of his attack, the rage of his invective, often evoked sympathy for the creeds upon which he trampled. Rational doubt is in accordance with the constitution of the human mind. Extremes meet—and doubt at length will turn upon and doubt itself!

Hubbard declared (too soon after Ingersoll) that Christianity had failed—that the churches were emptying—that the ministers would soon have to hunt other jobs. This he continued to repeat, with increasing bitterness of late years, from his own pulpit—for he too was a priest, though not according to the order of Melchisedek, and the title of honor dearest to his heart, as he confesses, was that of Teacher. The wise and thrifty Fra!!—all the ministers were going to lose their jobs, but he would keep his! Alas, the world is somewhat wider than East Aurora, and the heart of man has cravings that cannot be appeased by the Gospel of Roycroft.

It will be time enough to say that Christianity has

failed when once it has fairly been tried—the undying hope at the heart of humanity that it shall one day be so tried, is quite enough to warrant this religion as Divine. Again, only a fool or a dogmatist would deny that the Christian ethic, imperfectly as it is understood and lived up to, still remains the saving salt, the highest virtue of our civilization. In truth we are Christians, most of us, whether we go to church or not, and as it were, in despite of ourselves. There is no escape from it. In the time of Horace you had to be a pagan, though you might call yourself *parcus deorum cultor et infrequens.* In our time you have to be a Christian, though you make the same reservation. No man is great or strong enough to pull against the age.

And so Elbert Hubbard was a Christian, even after he parted with his dream of joining the ministry and stirring up the religious dry bones (my opinion is that in him the Rev. Billy Sunday narrowly escaped a dangerous rival). He ceased to go to church, but then he held church himself, and was an indefatigable preacher. Few persons have to search themselves so carefully on the subject of religion as the infidel who is required to justify his non-belief. Hubbard was always preoccupied with the religious idea—I really believe that literary inspiration aside, he would have been happier as a revivalist or exhorter of the most orthodox stamp. He wrote "The Man of Sorrows," a work that fully bears out this view of Elbert Hubbard, in spite of the crudely humanistic conception of JESUS which he is at pains to project. And it is only fair to add that he has traced many a page "on the side of the angels."

The fling at the ministers alluded to above is unworthy of Hubbard's naturally kind and tolerant spirit—it is indeed a weapon from the Ingersollian armory. Religious controversy does not make for sweetness and light, as we see in the record of both these amiable men. But we may regret it the more in the case of Elbert Hubbard, who was far less a born polemic than Colonel Ingersoll, and who had other gifts of more value to his generation and mayhap to times unborn. We heartily wish for him that he had kept out of that galley!

In his essay on the Book of Job, first published many years ago, Hubbard exposed a phase of his thought toward the great religious problems which seems to me far truer to his genius than the hard and repellant infidelity, the resigned and all but hopeless thanatism of his later years. He has been talking about the Book of Genesis, and he goes on to say in a charming digression:

"When I tell my little girl about the First Man and the First Woman who lived in a Beautiful Garden and were perfectly happy until they disobeyed God, she says, 'Oh, why didn't they mind what he said?' And then she throws her arms about my neck and assures me she will always do just what I wish her to do. So she confuses me with Deity and gives us the first hint of Ancestor Worship, for I am the biggest and strongest man she knows. . . .

"Some day I will tell her better. I shall not leave her to grope, and gain her knowledge of the most sacred and profound secrets of life from the lips of stupid ignorance and sin. And as the years go by and count themselves with the eternity that lies behind I shall not be here; and she will do as I have done and as you have done—stand by an open grave and ask in anguish, 'If a man die shall he live again?' And the falling clouds will give no sign, and the winds that sigh through the trees will make no reply; but Hope and Love will answer, Yes!"

Personally, I wish he had given us more of this mood, even if it would have kept down the varied output of the Roycroft Shops: I would trade a whole lot of the Gospel of Efficiency for it.

Perhaps I am not to be pitied for our estrangement,* in a way, as it gives me leave to recall the Elbert Hubbard of eighteen or twenty years ago—a quaintly romantic figure, with its bravado of long hair and eccentric costume; the dark magnetic eye with its hint of power, the mobile face, a little stern, that yet easily yielded to mirth. If it were not too fantastic, I would almost say, a blend of Alfred Jingle and Robert Louis the Beloved. His smile was very beautiful in those days: both men and women readily yielded to its fascinating charm.

The portrait prefixed to the essays which in book-form he called "As it Seems to Me" (edition of 1898) is the man as I like best to recall him. The pose and *réclame* of later pictures are happily wanting; his hair scarcely falls below the collar, and his necktie is of conventional size and pattern. But the likeness is a very fine and true one—it long holds

* See Chapter, "A Footnote," pp. 206 ff.

the gaze of one who can go back to the original of thirty years ago. The face is handsome, aquiline, and the atmosphere about it seems to project one of the "devoted":—there is, as it were, a veritable hunger of passion and purpose upon it. (I have already noted my partiality for this book as offering some of his finest pages.)

The dreamer was then uppermost in Elbert Hubbard, and with due praise for his practical achievement, it is as a dreamer that he will be longest remembered.

"The dreamer lives forever, but the toiler dies in a day."

Yes, Elbert Hubbard was a dreamer, and his dream remains in the "Little Journeys" and a hundred essays of a blended humor and pathos, tenderness and strength, entirely his own.

This man owed little to the schools and nothing to the dead languages, but he was master of a vocabulary that was most intensely alive and as copious as Mark Twain's. He was one of the great workers of America, but not too busy, and he never had time to whisper in his own left ear that he was a genius.

Another great worker of our time, Bernard Shaw, with whom as a writer and thinker Elbert Hubbard had not a little in common, has thus defined his attitude toward life:

> "This is the true joy in life, the being used for a purpose recognized by yourself as a mighty one; the being thoroughly worn out before you are thrown on the scrap-heap; the being a force of Nature instead of a feverish, selfish little clod of ailments and grievances complaining that the world will not devote itself to making you happy."

Elbert Hubbard might have written these words, so true are they to his own faith and philosophy. Equally notable is his creed that "the reward which life holds out for work is not idleness nor rest, nor immunity from work, but increased capacity, GREATER DIFFICULTIES, MORE WORK." No man ever spared himself less. No man ever made a fuller use of his powers and energies. As he was at thirty-five, so he was at fifty-five; he seems never to have relaxed the pace, but rather to have bettered it in point of efficiency and productive effort.

I want to say a word about his general competency as a writer,—not indeed that such a word is needed by the intelligent, but in view of the sneering suspicion voiced in certain quarters that he was not what is called a liberally educated man. The said suspicion being confined, mark you, to certain persons who could not write like him for their lives.

That sneer of envy and impotency at genius and power,—is it not one of the oldest things in the world? As old at least as the first dunce whom the college sent home, a gold brick, to his proud parents.

Yes, that sneer is about the only visible advantage some people derive from a college education.

A college which would grant a diploma without conferring the inalienable right of educated duncery to sneer at its betters, would surely never thrive in our country.

The barren womb and the brain cultivated but sterile are two things hard to satisfy.

In the course of a tribute to his friend, Stephen Crane—one of the earliest and most famous of the Roycrofters—Elbert Hubbard said:

"Stephen Crane was an artist in his ability to convey the feeling by just the right word, or a word misplaced, like a lady's dress in disarray, or a hat askew. This daring quality marks everything he wrote. The recognition that language is fluid and at best only an expedient, flavors all his work. He makes no fetich of grammar—if grammar gets in the way so much the worse for the grammar. All is packed with color and charged with feeling: yet the work is usually quiet in quality and modest in manner."

Men like Elbert Hubbard rise to their best self-valuation in estimating the effort of kindred souls. These words written of Stephen Crane are equally true of himself—a clean sharp outline of his artistic creed and a just measure of his literary responsibility. It is a perfect self-portrait, and we see that in literature as in practical life the great word with him was Efficiency. This is the mark of all his better, more deliberate work. There is no redundancy or writing for the sake of writing: the man has always something to say, and if it is not always something new, be sure he will say it with an emphasis and point that make it his own. The cleanly processes of this man's mind, the freedom from literary pose and artifice, are of themselves distinctive and alluring. The highest virtue of his style was, I think, his simple and always perfectly successful aim to share his thought with the reader.

The School of Literary Obfuscation has followers in some exalted places, but of these was not Elbert Hubbard. I'm sure it would be impossible to convict him of having written even a single sentence whose meaning was not clear to himself.* Whatever fate may be in store for his literary legacy, we can be sure that societies will never be formed to study and expound his works. His tongue was in his cheek always for the sort of greatness that requires such interpretation.

Elbert Hubbard had the misfortune—which he shares with some of the world's greatest writers—not to have been a college-bred man. He knew no languages save his own. This point as to his literary equipment is worth our notice, for, as I have said, it is made much of in depreciating him by certain snobbish persons who cannot write in any language.

* I do not extenuate the solecisms and slips in ordinary scholarship which disfigure too many of his pages and which have prejudiced his work in the eyes of the critical. A good proofreader would have saved all that.

Joseph McCabe, in his valuable study of Bernard Shaw, makes a similar note in regard to that famous writer. Mr. Shaw, it seems, is innocent of Latin and Greek and is likewise guiltless of the modern tongues, save French and a little German.

McCabe who was bred for the Church and is himself an erudite scholar, regrets that the author of "Man and Superman" was not properly ballasted with the old classic learning. Evidently he thinks it would have had the useful effect of holding the volatile Bernard Shaw down and curtailing his erratic excursions in the realm of whimsical satire or topsy-turvy economics. However, he makes the important admission that this very lack on the part of Shaw gives the greater vitality to his work: in other words, makes him more efficient in his appeal to the present generation. Ah! there we have it.

The classical scholar, you know, is bound to have one eye on the past and one eye on the present. Now the alert and sagacious Bernard never lets go his audience for a minute, and in the best of his plays he is contemporaneous to the second.

I wonder if it has not been a very fair exchange for him!

On this point Hubbard and Shaw are again in agreement. Both lovers of efficiency, ascetic as to their personal appetites, but liberal in their publicly professed moral code, acute judges of themselves and shrewd appraisers of other men, preternaturally gifted opportunists, with a special talent for success—they refused to store their brains with the learned lumber of the past. And Hubbard wrote:

"Linguists are seldom thinkers. . . . My opinion is that to master the language of Shakespeare is quite ambition enough for the average man. If you speak several languages you will probably speak none of them well."

Shaw has said, you remember, that a man fully capable of the resources of his own tongue will not bother with a foreign language.

Finally Hubbard sums up his mind as to this matter in a memorable conclusion:

"I make no plea for the indictment of any man who affects languages dead or living; but I modestly protest that simplicity, truthfulness, mental self-reliance, physical health, and the education of

ELBERT HUBBARD

the hand as well as brain, shall not be left out of the accounting when we make our formula for a man."

It cannot be said that the difficulty has been entirely settled for us by either Shaw or Hubbard (personally I may own to a liking for a little of the She-Wolf's milk), but the courage and example of both these masterful men will surely help us to a solution.

For themselves I have no doubt that circumstances, as well as their own choice, worked for their success. A writer can be handicapped by too much scholarship or mere verbal equipment—we know how Flaubert was clogged and impeded by his learning, and why his "St. Anthony" is a *via crucis* even to the scholar.

After all, what are words—words—words! The living brain and heart outweigh all the tomes of the dead and dusty past. Let us not forget, too, that excessive culture makes for dilettanteism—for insincerity.

Elbert Hubbard was well equipped for his work:

his pen was as a lance that, like a knight at a tourney, he wielded with careless ease. None that ever faced him in the combat had a right to sneer at his weapon, and upon its glittering blade was never seen the smirch of blood unfairly shed!

William Morris, the many-sided Englishman, was the man of modern times whom Elbert Hubbard most loved and admired.

The fact is illuminating. Consciously we choose those whom we would resemble—whose dream answers to ours.

In all his better effort Morris was confessedly his model and inspiration, and it is not too much to say that without the Kelmscott Press and other kindred enterprises, the Roycroft and its community would never have been called into existence.

And the conditions were very unequal as between Morris and his American follower. Let us see a little.

William Morris was born to wealth, in the midst of an old civilization, and enjoyed the advantages of an English University education—these advantages are not to be denied, especially when you get a mind capable of both utilizing and resisting what the colleges give.

He was free to do as he pleased. He never felt the hand of a task-master on his shoulder.

There was no loss of time in getting his equipment. And he got it easily, painlessly in the receptive season of youth, taught by the best masters, inspired by the emulation of his fellows, encouraged and applauded by all. He never knew the terrible pains and sacrifices which the seeker of knowledge must pay for lost years and opportunities denied.

Leaving the university with honor, his mind stored with all the rich spoil of the ages, he could justly say that he was lord of his own life and master of his future.

The career of Elbert Hubbard offers a harsh contrast to that of the more fortunate Englishman.

He was born in a crude society and was brought up in an environment hostile to those dreams which are the nursing milk of the future artist.

His early schooling was limited in extent and short in duration.

He was thrown into the battle of life at a tender

age, and he knew no college save the University of Hard Knocks, where he gave as good an account of himself as the next one.

Always he cherished a dream of the intellectual life, and having by great ability and strenuous labor amassed a competency in his early thirties—no small achievement that, if you please—he took up his true vocation, and he was not far from forty when he set his hand to the work that has made him famous.

Really, an astonishing career, viewed with sympathy and understanding.

If he did not become the William Morris of America it was only because of the handicaps which fate threw against him from his earliest years. But perhaps it was quite enough to have made himself Elbert Hubbard!

I have said that Hubbard gives us the clue to his own self-estimation when he writes upon Stephen Crane. Even more significant and valuable in this light is his appreciation of William Morris—the one man of the moderns whom he was proud to call his leader. It is Elbert Hubbard confessing Elbert Hubbard *via* William Morris. He says:

"William Morris thought literature should be the product of the ripened mind—the mind that knows the world of men and has grappled with earth's problems. . . . He considered that literature should not be a profession in itself—to make a business of art is to degrade it.

"Literature should be the spontaneous output of the mind that has known and felt. To work the mine of spirit as a business and sift its products for hire, is to overwork the vein and palm off slag for useful metal."

Hubbard liked to describe himself as a printer or farmer—not as a writer. He would even romance a bit in order to evade the literary imputation, and we know why. Because, as he says, "Shakespeare was a theatre manager, Milton a secretary, Burns a farmer, Lamb a book-keeper, Wordsworth a Government employee, Whitman a clerk, and William Morris was a working man and manufacturer."

His tribute to Morris is fine and memorable. I quote again:

"The man who could influence the entire housekeeping of half a world and give the kingdom of fashion a list to starboard; who could paint beautiful pictures; compose music; speak four languages; address a public assembly effectively; produce plays, resurrect the lost art of making books—books such as were made only in the olden time as a loving, religious service; who lived a clean, wholesome, manly life—beloved by those who knew him best—shall we not call him Master?"

Again I see Hubbard more than Morris behind these noble, fitting words: his noblest ambition, his constant inspiration is written there.

It is true there are some people, critics and censors of the man, who think he relaxed in his ambition and came tardy off in his performance. They assert that he renounced his old idealism, which had won him his first and better following, shuffled with his principles, and bent the knee to Baal.

I am not concerned to try the issue, but I believe that summing up this man's life-work as a whole, the future will pronounce a fairer and kindlier judgment.

The career of this man is one of the romances of our time, and the dazzlement of it is still in our eyes, so that we cannot as yet justly measure Elbert Hubbard or his work. It is a stern romance too, and one after the American heart; inspiring with its lesson of handicaps overcome and difficulties surmounted, of heroïc reliance upon self, of many a hard-fought battle and not a few superb victories. I am utterly persuaded that it owed little or nothing to accident.

Practically unknown at forty, Elbert Hubbard became within a few years a national figure. The development of his talent—or I should say talents—was I think both exceptional as to men of his type and extraordinary in itself. Something of this was due to the continence and wisdom which he had preserved even from boyhood. Unlike most men of the artistic impulse, he had wasted nothing in youth, and so maturity was to him but the unsealing of the wells of power. I believe he never came to know and suffer the first symptom of decadence or loss of power—at least I can find no evidence of it in the latest work of his pen.

I said just now that there was something exceptional in the late unfolding of his abilities. Let me make my meaning plainer—it seems worth the trouble. When I first met him he was well up in his thirties, and he gave his lectures with much charm;

always, however, reading from his manuscript. One does not often hear of a man who made himself a ready and powerful speaker after forty. Elbert Hubbard did this and so achieved equal facility with voice and pen.

It is hard to bring the writing brain and the talking brain to do team work, but sometimes it can be done, and the results justify our homage to power and versatility.

Of course it is as a writer that he interests me most, and that, as I believe, his fame will long endure. I have lately looked over a great part of his work, and I must honestly avow that I think better of it than ever before.

He has been accused of stealing much from other pens (I have myself broken a lance with him in this quarrel), but at worst his plagiarizing seems to have been unethical rather than felonious.* I wish he had let it alone; it extended only to words and phrases, mere verbal borrowings, rather than to ideas—no one has ever charged him with a poverty of ideas. There is not enough weight in all his alleged plagiarisms to impeach his credit as an orig-

* See "A Footnote," pp. 206 ff.

inal writer and thinker. But it must be allowed that in this matter his Yankee smartness served him an ill turn—the bit of stolen pinchbeck often makes his whole cargo suspect.

The truth is, Hubbard never could be got to take literature *per se* as seriously as those who neither took nor cared to take anything else, and hence his lack of squeamishness in the matter of "assimilation"—it by no means argued a sterility or want of original power on his part. Always to him writing was a means to an end rather than the end itself—as it is to a writer of pure literary motive. Here was a province in which his passion for Efficiency led him astray—it seemed so easy to take what was already pat to his hand! For this he has been censured far beyond the measure of his offending.

Perhaps a worse thing for his future fame was the flippant ignorance he sometimes displayed in regard to matters that asked from him a wise discretion. This is only to say that if he had possessed knowledge equal to his courage and ability, he would have been a very great man indeed. But he never claimed infallibility for himself, and he would not allow it to any man born of woman.

As a writer he permitted himself many freedoms which shocked and continue to shock the Dryasdust School of literary expression: but he never allowed himself to be dull. Ah! that is perhaps what gives them most offence.

He had wit and personality *plus,* the value of which was accentuated by a keen and sage philosophy of life and an exquisite sense of the practical—so often left out of the mere literary man.

He wrote with a courage too often denied the literary artist struggling with adversity—a courage that sprang from his having beaten the world at its own game. Of his literary style he forged a perfect weapon that was now a whip of scorpions for his foes and the things he hated, and again for those who knew and understood him, a golden arrow tipped with love.

Hamlet and Puck strove equally within him for expression—this is the recipe by which you shall hold the world's ear and for which the Tribe of Dunces will eternally hate you!

Elbert Hubbard wrote a great many books—I don't know how many and I know still less how he found time to do it—but every one of them can be read, and some indeed are eminently valuable—they form an addition to our permanent literature.

But all this is but a partial truth and an incomplete measure of the man. We have all felt that there was something in him greater than his written word—such men as he cannot reveal their secret. Strong as was his literary appeal, he was more than a writer—and all that we see about us is but the shadow of his dream.

Death struck him, envious and sudden as the lightning, in the fulness of his powers—powers of body and mind, nourished by manly self-denial and strengthened by success upon success. And though so brief the space since he left us, we see that Time has already begun to do him justice. To many who somewhat impatiently judged him, his life and work now appear of a singular and valid consistency. Errors there were, unavoidable in the earth-passage of such a spirit, but these were gloriously redeemed by his valiant stand for right and truth, for liberty and justice, as he recognized them. This is the side of Elbert Hubbard's shield which will gain the battle for him—the side he uplifted to receive the rays of the dawn!

I know it has been alleged that in much of his precept and practice he was no true pioneer of progress but an echo of the great voices that have in the past spoken for liberty of conscience and the rights of humanity.

Without granting this contention, let us be glad that his critics concede so much, for when such echoes die out entirely, then you shall see all manner of old slaveries and superstitions creeping back into the world.

He was a new force in the struggle for liberty that must be waged eternally if we are to keep it, and as such, whatever his errors and excesses, his work remains of great value. But his highest praise, perhaps, and the praise that he would have been gladdest of, is that by word and example he gave meaning and purpose to thousands of lives. He was a Master of Life, and he presented the novel and inspiring spectacle of a Soul in Business! His practical philosophy, his ethics for the conduct of man's "little journey" in the world, were as sound as Franklin's and of much greater literary charm. His preachments on business and success, on the relations of employer and employee, and kindred themes, were full of a keenness and good sense peculiar to the man; they were very widely diffused and had an extraordinary influence. Herein he has a title to remembrance which we can be sure will not soon be effaced.

* * * * * * *

It is the man I knew and loved, the friend of my youth, the *bon camarade,* the melancholy *Jaques* of our lighter literature, as rare a spirit as ever wore the motley, whom I have tried to picture for you as he will ever exist for me. May I not say that I esteem it as a privilege to remember him in the light of those vanished years when friendship was as precious and perturbing as love itself—when the heart gave of its fulness and kept no record of its bounty—when the Dream and the Glory were the dearer that it lured us both!

I said a little while ago that coming in on the train I could not help feeling that I was about to meet him, as of yore, when I made my pleasant pilgrimages to East Aurora. The air seemed vibrant and electric with the old friendship. A hand waved familiar greeting from a cloud. I was thrilled with something of the old expectation. And here in this atmosphere of love, among those of his blood and the wider circle of his friends and admirers,—all you who rightly think of him as not dead but living in a life more potential,—I am fain to believe that we have had our meeting and our reconciliation.

## DIABOLUS

SCENE: East Aurora. TIME: The present.

The Roycroft buildings, massive, red-tiled and turreted, stand up bravely in the sun, though the Mind that evoked them into being has returned to the Infinite Thought.

But there is no change in the ordered life and industry of the place. Still, as obedient to the Master's will, all seems to move as before the Great Catastrophe. The whir of the printing presses can be heard from the Shop. The workers are busy at their several tasks. Some young people are playing ball and tennis on the grounds: they too are workers and their play is a permitted relaxation. Country Hebes, plump and pink-cheeked, flutter to and fro in cool muslin; young men in jerseys add their robust health to the picture. To the stranger this idyllic setting of an industrial enterprise seems hardly credible; some little time is required to perceive that behind the charming *mise en scène* is the unchangeable reality of work and wages.

Men are mowing the smooth lawns or tidying the flower-bordered walks, keeping up that seemliness the Master loved and which he insisted upon in all things. Everywhere a wise economy of effort and a certain demure regard to appearances. Why not? Granted the obvious intention as to much of this, is it any the less true that to make labor lovely and desirable for its own sake, is one of the noblest ends for which men may strive? . . . There's a plenty of guests at the Inn and visitors can be seen wending their way between the several buildings. All as of yore.

Not quite, for the air lacks a vital something—the emanation of that Personality to which all that we see was but lately the mere frame or background. It is in fact next to impossible to *realize* the place without HIM. The problem instantly poses itself——

But at this fortuitous moment I almost fall over the Genius.

Part of his angular disjointed length sprawls over the sidewalk as he slouches in a sitting posture against the fence. He presents a flagrant antithesis of the cleverly devised Poem of Labor before our eyes: it is the Alpha and Omega of contrast; antipodes of sentiment that swear at each other in strident blasphemies. It is morning and, as I have said, the hum of industry rises about us. But the Genius is in a state of perfect equilibrium and inertia: he is resting. And if it is good to rest in the evening, why not in the morning? Answer me that!

The Genius salutes me without getting up or otherwise discommoding himself, and then with a significant leer that comprehends the whole scene before us, he remarks: "Well, he's dead."

"Yes," I assent, a little surprised at the triteness of the remark from a Genius; "and a great pity it is."

"Oh, I don't refer to his personal dissolution or evanescence," he rejoins somewhat hastily (for him).

"What, then?" I probe as he again paused, feeling doubtless that such animation was not in character.

"Why, of course I mean the stuff he wrote and printed over there"—(with an ineffable grimace)—"his message, you know, and all that. You didn't imagine it would live, eh? He knew himself it wouldn't—that wistful look of his, you remember—it's in a lot of his pictures—was directed at the posterity he will never reach. Ah, you can't 'con' posterity!"

Here the Genius crosses his sprawling legs in a loathly fashion, and relieves himself of a "Humph" of sardonic emphasis.

I think of the Devil's Advocate who pleads against those proposed for the honors of sainthood or immortality. The Genius is sufficiently like a devil or an *Advocatus Diaboli*. He looks at me slyly with half closed exotic eyes, and I feel that he is meditating an epigram.

It was plain that he, the Genius—the reckless, the irresponsible one, the Failure—exulted over the eventual defeat of the Man of Talent and industry, the strenuous Builder of Success.

I shuddered as I read this bitter thought in his narrowed eyes, and I could not be sure if he had spoken the words aloud.

"I am an artist: I must hate as an artist," went on this man who had achieved nothing that the world honors as success.

Bravely, defiantly, the Roycroft's turreted structures uplifted their shoulders in the sun; they are made of stone that will outlast the hills, I said to myself (as fearing that this glowering Demon would hear me). The cheerful sounds of labor rise on all hands, and hark, what is that?—the Roycroft girls are singing at their work. All this because a brave Man toiled and thought!

"But you see," riposts the Genius, interpreting my thought, "if he was right, then *we* are wrong!"

At this I broke into inextinguishable laughter.

"So of course he can't live, you know," he interjected half-pleadingly.

But I only laughed the more.

What a pipe it was! What a masterpiece of unconscious irony!

"Yes, and all that too will pass," he spat forth angrily, indicating the shops with a sweeping hostile gesture. "Do you think it can live upon the Shadow of a Shadow? That the Show can go on without the Showman?"

I checked my laughter then, a little sobered.

But the sun continued to shine gayly, triumphantly on the turreted strength of the Roycroft.

## A FOOTNOTE

IT was my misfortune to have been estranged from Elbert Hubbard many years ago. Really I have forgotten why: the causes were of no account: when do they ever seem important, viewed through the annulling glass of time? I do not pretend to have been without fault in the matter. It was easier for me to see red in those days than it is now. But the quarrel was actively served and diligently promoted by our common friends:—I suspect the hearts of the principals were never much in it. It was a very pretty quarrel, however, fed by mischievous tongues and eagerly ministered to by the creatures of envy, hatred and jealousy. There was bitter talk and counter-talk which the common friends traded back and forth with a quite incredible alacrity, never forgetting to dot and carry one in the process.

I loved Elbert Hubbard during the several years of our close friendship, which began almost with the birth of the "Philistine." And though we fell out at length, owing to causes which seem foolish enough to my better judgment, and though we were never really reconciled, to the extent of a personal meeting, I have never hated the man. How could I hate one who seemed to share the ideals of my youth—a friend with whom I have laughed and held communion in the things of the mind?

It is not for me to say how much sympathy there was between us. Perhaps indeed our friendship failed on this very account—the point does not matter now; and I remember only the good hours of that friendship and regret that the page is turned forever.

As noted in the text, Hubbard was rather late in coming to literature—he had stopped on the way to pick up an honest fortune in a strictly commercial industry, which experience stamped his whole subsequent career. No reproach in this surely, but the Fra was needlessly concerned to suppress it, preoccupied always with the construction of a fitting legend, and he at times romanced extravagantly in order to hide the real facts of his early career. He used to tell a yarn of his life as a cowboy in the west, which part he dressed very well, having furnished himself with a regular broncho buster's outfit to make the thing good. I remember I once laughed at this when he had given a rehearsal for my special behoof in his barn at East Aurora. He never quite forgave it me. Artists are so sensitive!

In the fact of his late coming to literature may be found some extenuation of his most grievous offending as a writer. Perhaps no man that ever wielded a pen has been so persistently, and not seldom unjustly, accused of stealing the thoughts and even the expressions of others. Truth is, the Fra never could acquire a due respect for quotation marks; never could see the iniquity and, in the long run, the suicidal error of purloining the fruit of another man's brain. All authorship is, of course, more or less derivative, and it has been the boast of some great writers—Heine for example—that they took their own wherever they found it. But this is a species of appropriation justified by genius alone, and literature is the richer for it where that which was filched is doubled in grace and value. Such was

Heine's idea when he declared that there was no Sixth Commandment in Art—to justify the practice of a Shakespeare, not to make a brief for the Artful Dodgers of literature.

## WALT WHITMAN—TWO NOTES

### I

IF there were any avowed obscenity in Whitman—anything worse than the plainness of the honest word uttered with the poet's high purpose—his fame would owe far less than it does to the sympathy of women. Even so it must be something of a stumbling block to them. But indeed I have always held that women in these matters are more honest than men—perhaps I should say *a certain kind of men,* the kind that would profess themselves purer than other men's mothers and sisters.

Even so, I do not myself believe that the "Leaves of Grass" is the best possible book to put into the hands of an *ingenue,* as I have heard enthusiastic votaries of Whitman declare; I do not expect to bring up my children on it. Neither do I give them the key to that infamous history of lust and slaughter which is contained in the Holy Bible, that divine Book by which alone we can be saved. I

WALT WHITMAN

should not like to have them ask me, in their innocence, what it was that the men of the plain sought to do with Lot's angelic visitors when they fought in their blindness about the doorposts. I should not care to have to expound for them the chaste romance of the daughters of Lot; or the pathetic history of the Levite and his concubine in the nineteenth chapter of Judges. I would hate to have them press me hard as to the reason why Uriah was left to die in the front of battle—yes, it would pain me very much to have to show up the real character of that lustful, murderous egoist who describes himself as a lamb that the Lord his shepherd leads by still waters!

Then there is that crowning atrocity of lust and blood, the book of Esther—how could I bear to see my children turning those lurid pages,—even though the guilt and the shame were not for them to feel! Or smearing their minds in the vile passages of the Pentateuch? Or rejoicing at the rescue of the guilty harlot Rahab, while an innocent people perished at the bidding of the Lord? Or singing with Deborah the praise of that other harlot and murderess, Jael?

Truly if it came to a choice I think, after all, that I should prefer to put into my children's hands the "Leaves of Grass"—there would be so much less to explain! . . .

## II

Walt Whitman's fame was of the kind that would have justified and no doubt inspired an attractive "legend," had it been left to make itself, without meddling of fools or notoriety-hunters, for a decent interval after his death. Unluckily for old Walt, he fell in during his later years with the amiable but lethally industrious Traubel, who in "boswellizing" Whitman has extended the known limits of human stupidity. It is not too much to say that he has almost buried Walt under a mountain of rubbish—and up to the end he kept everlastingly at it with barrow and shovel and pick!

Terrible has been the result of that misguided industry. Any person of ordinary powers of endurance who sees Traubel first will never survive to reach Whitman. There is something stupefying in the complacency which the Disciple exhibited in turning out his endless volumes of folderol. He has killed off or for long discouraged all hope or chance of a fitting legend by his wearisome exposition of Whitman's vast ignorance, provincial narrowness, amazing lack of taste, puerile prejudices and, finally, his inordinate, even fetid, self-conceit. I know it has been suggested, but I do not believe, that the Disciple, in the weird processes of his "art," has transferred these his own personal qualities to the Master; thus, the hybrid changeling he gives us may be one part Whitman to three parts Traubel. The thing is not without precedent, as we know. But I am at least sure of this—he has projected a Whitman who fails utterly to live up to the best and highest in the "Leaves"; an unlovely, repellent, hideously egotistical chatterer (one thinks how awful it must have been to endure all that frouzy gossip!); a pontificating old palaverer, with scarcely a trace of the nobility of letters about him.

How Emerson would have revolted at the frequent, ungraceful lugging in of his name to support the Whitman self-puffery!—there is all too much greasy offence of this sort, which has its natural effect on the sensitive reader. . . .

Isaac Hull Platt has done a book on Walt Whitman, without foolishness,—a rare thing! No poet was ever more damned in his eulogists and imitators—these latter especially—than old Walt. They would have brought a smaller man into everlasting contempt, and, no question, they repel many who would otherwise seek him. So there is uncommon reason to be grateful for this good book of Dr. Platt's, written in clean terse English (a tongue unknown to several windy Whitmanites) and offering a competent sketch of the poet's life, with a sane appreciation of his work. Dr. Platt is a scholar and therefore does not sicken us with praise of Whitman's solecisms and vulgarities—he points us to his great qualities. Whitman's lack of regular poetic form makes him easily imitable, as to his fourth-rate stuff, by mediocre or bad poets, and a number of such feeble yawpers have colonized on his great fame, like lice on a dead lion. But he is not the less certainly one of the few immortals this country has produced, and you may not pass him by. . . .

Someone has asked me, by the way, to name the

poem or passage of Whitman's that I like best. Well, the choice is not easy, for I have several favorites, although Whitman has to be taken all of a piece, and is not a poet for the anthologies. But the following lines seem to me among the most remarkable that old Walt ever penned,—those especially which attest the freedom and originality of his mind, and rank him with the Great Worthies of literature:

I think I could turn and live with animals, they are so placid and self-contained;
I stand and look at them long and long.
They do not sweat and whine about their condition,
They do not lie awake in the dark and weep for their sins,
They do not make me sick discussing their duty to God.
Not one is dissatisfied, not one is demented with the mania of owning things,
Not one kneels to another, nor to his kind that lived thousands of years ago,
Not one is respectable or unhappy over the whole earth.

## THE FIRST EURAMERICAN

THE other day I picked up at a second-hand book stall, "Lotus-Eating" by George William Curtis; imprint of the Harpers, date 1852. I took the little volume home and read it with a curious interest, not on account of any merit in the work, but mainly for that it was the production of George William Curtis.

I wonder if the Class in Literature could tell us anything about him? Probably not, though he bulked large among his contemporaries, wrote several books and was one of the great men at Harpers' when that famous house stood without a rival—the substance of a mighty name.

George William was the first of our literary men to part his hair in the middle and the last to wear whiskers. He recalls the "Keepsake" era, to which he in part belonged, with its literary artificialities and *fade* sentiment. He was something of a dandy, and there is a suggestion of the d'Orsay pose in his earlier portraits. Also he was of a personality not unpleasing to the ladies, and his "literature" did no violence to their powers of appreciation. His connection with the Harpers (he long edited the "Monthly") and his "literary works" gave him a prestige which at first blush is not easy to understand. That indeed explains why I bought his book; it was an early production of his, I knew, and I wished to study him at the source.

I found the book entertaining for what it told or suggested of George William and for the answer it made to the conundrum of his fame and success. The author, thus early, posed as a *Euramerican* (if I may coin the word) and affected a superior tone in writing of and to his fellow countrymen. He loads his pages with exotic quotation and observation; tells you of his foreign travels when his business is to describe the Hudson and the Catskills; insinuates disparagement of America and things American with or without pretext; minces like a man-milliner and often moralizes like a Turveydrop (see especially the chapter on Saratoga). Intellectually he has succeeded in denationalizing himself and is almost confessedly proud of the fact, yet he never fails to betray himself as an American snob of the first water. It is written across this book from the first page, when he ambles forth on his travels with Herrick's poems under his arm, to the last when he bids farewell to Newport in some pretty trifling verses; it peeps out in his sentimental reflections; it is lugged in at every turn and on the slightest occasion. But for all that we should be grateful—if it were not for George William's snobbery we should never be able to get through his book!

Along with this temperamental and spiritual quality there goes a "preciousness" of style that here and there marks some very amusing effects. For his artificial soul and his factitious personality George William had invented an entirely adequate style. But with all his anxious display of exotic haberdashery he can not write, save as an amateur. It may well amaze the Class in Literature that a writer of George William's fame could have turned out such twaddle as this (of which "Lotus-Eating" offers not a few examples):

"Not four days away from the city, I have not yet done roaming, bewildered with the summer's breath, through the garden, smelling of all the flowers and returning to lie upon the lawn, and bask, dreaming in the July sun. What a cold word is 'beautiful' to express the 'ecstacy' which, in some choice moments of midsummer, suddenly overwhelms your mind, like an unexpected and exquisite thought!"

George William is very careful never to "overwhelm" us in the manner described, but he often diverts us with specimens of the following curiously labored and affected expression:

"A sharp-faced, thought-furrowed, hard-handed American, with his anxious eye and sallow complexion, his nervous motion and concentrated expression, and withal, accoutred for travelling in blue coat with gilt buttons, dark pantaloons, patent leather boots, and silk vest hung with charms, chains and bits of metal, as if the Indian love of lustre lingered in the Yankee, is not unlike one of these steamers whose machinery, driving it along, jars the cut glass and the choice centre-tables and crimson-covered lounges, and with a like accelerated impetus would shiver the filigree into splinters."

I don't know what George William is driving at in this paragraph, but I do know it is a fair example of the literary talent exhibited in "Lotus-Eating," which the Harpers made into a book in the year

1852. (By the way, in that very year while George William aired his superior culture and labored his esthetic fancies about the Hudson, etc., a shambling boy at Hannibal, Mo., was looking for a job on a steamboat and preparing himself to write the prose epic of the Mississippi. Lucky for us that Mark Twain arrived to save us from the tribe of George William.) It may console some aspiring beginners who have not yet been able to get published, that the above quoted abuse of type and paper was perpetrated in the name of Literature!

In the old books of rhetoric that we studied in my youth there were given examples of the *True* and the *False Sublime,* to the end that we might learn to identify and accurately differentiate them in our compositions. I can tell the Class in Literature that it is not every day one chances upon so rare and perfect a specimen of the *False Sublime* as this which I here cull from George William:

"When I was on the Faulhorn, the highest point in Europe upon which a dwelling house is placed, and that inhabited for only three months in the year, I stepped out in the middle of the night, and as I looked across the valley of Grindelwald and saw the snow-fields and ice-precipices of all the Horns—never trodden and never to be trodden by man—shining cold in the moonlight, my heart stood still as I felt that those awful peaks and I were alone in the solemn solitude. Then I felt the significance of Switzerland, and knew the sublimity of mountains."

If the Alps are conscious (as Turgenev imagines, in one of his prose fancies) then it must have been an equally thrilling moment for them when they found themselves alone with George William!

The literary style of this long admired author reminds one of nothing so much as the "skeleton" dress suit which undertakers provide for their defunct clients—all front and no back. He was not the inventor of it, even in this country (there was his prototype, the elegant and dandiacal N. P. Willis), but I think he "got across" with it (as we say now) more successfully than any other of our literati. This is distinction of a sort; and at very least it assures George William a place among the curiosities of the printed word.

(The reader is warned against taking this little depreciation too seriously, since there be moods in which we think more kindly of George William and his literary legacy—other portions of it, to be sure. But if he still refuses to smile at our irreverent handling of a former Idol, and if it be allowable to bring unequal things into comparison, let him turn to Mark Twain's "revaluation" of the great Fenimore Cooper.)

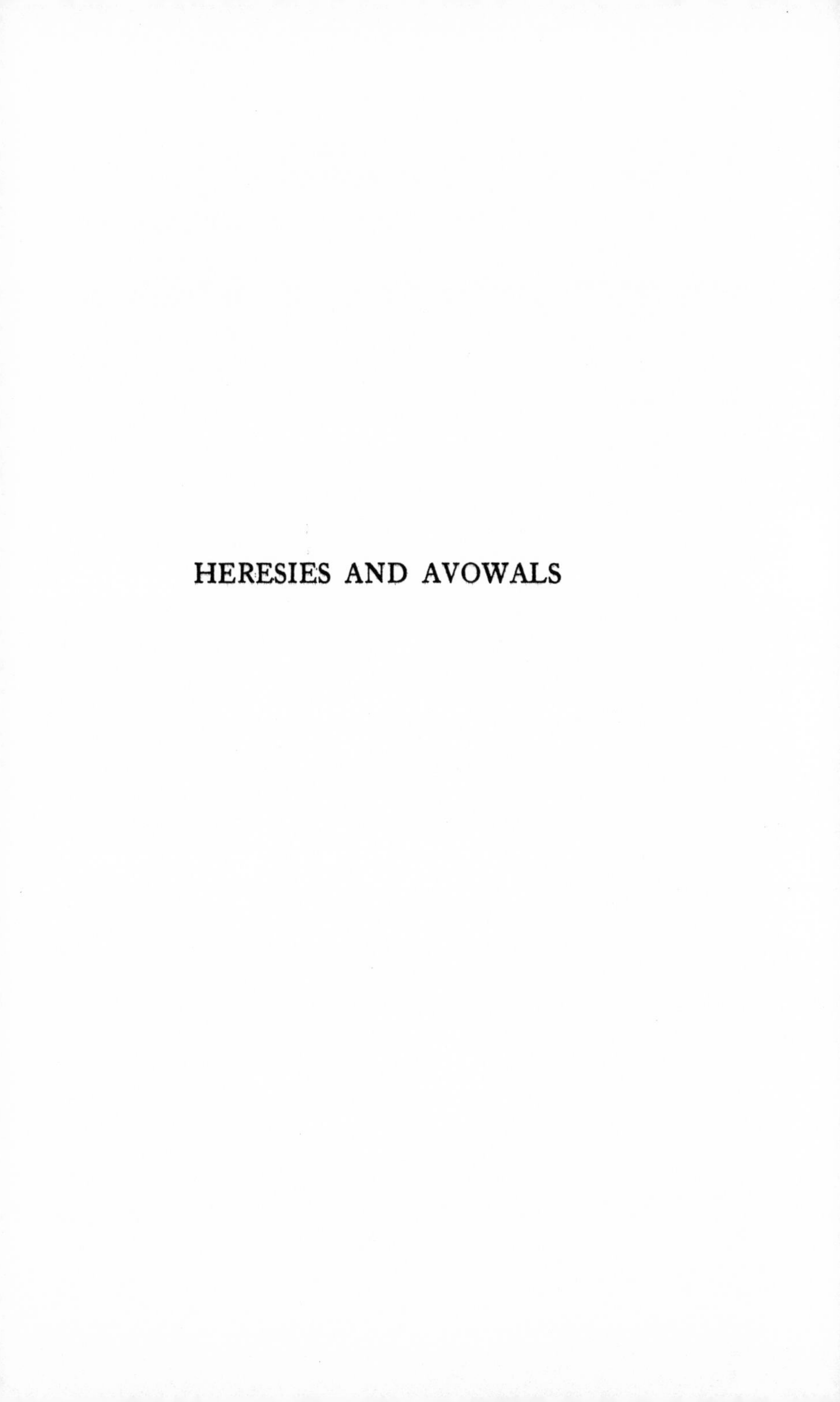

# HERESIES AND AVOWALS

## ORIGINALITY

NOTHING is more common than to speak of some new writer as "original." The person so speaking never thinks that he is declaring a miracle. And the marvel is usually allowed to pass unchallenged.

Now true originality in literature has not been possible during some centuries. Strictly speaking, to say that a new writer is original, is to accuse him of having read nothing, for on no other terms could he achieve originality. One can hardly form a phrase without summoning in aid the "delicate Ariel" of memory, and the best an honest writer can do is to write without consciously stealing or *remembering*—very few put so fine a point on it. "I'll example you with thievery" says Shakespeare, in a famous passage,—

> "The sun's a thief and with his great attraction
> Robs the vast sea; the moon's an arrant thief
> And her pale fire she snatches from the sun."

He might have exampled us with his own practice, for no genius of the first order was ever so much indebted to others, a writer of his own time calling him "a daw dressed in our plumage," or words to the same effect. Since this is true of the sovereign of English literature, it is rather difficult to piece out how his successors and copyists have made shift for originality.

Of American writers, Emerson, regarded as our most original thinker, can hardly offer a page that is not a labored mosaic of imitation, quotation and reminiscence. Thrifty persons read him to refresh themselves as to his originals.

All the stories have been told over and over and over again; all the rhymes coupled so often that even syllables bear the stamp of repeated plagiarism; all the ideas worked out to utter weariness of iteration. Strike the Grand Lyre of literature: it returns only an echo. Life the Perfumed Bowl of poetic wassail: hot lips have been before thee draining the last dregs.

There are still some virtues left in the writing trade, but of these is not originality.

## THE SHADOW IN THE HOUSE

ONE of the strangest ironies of life is the good health that attends the fool. By the fool I mean a type of person peculiarly fatal to his or her kindred; author of obscure tragedies from which the world bleeds in secret.

Nature has some occult purpose in providing the fool with sound physical health, and indeed lacking this, he (or she) could not be successful in his vocation; which is to make havoc in other lives. Here as elsewhere it seems possible to convict Nature of a malevolent design.

If I could have but one wish I would ask for the wisdom of the wise and the strength of the fool!

Who does not know of a family whose peace and happiness are constantly broken by the vicious folly of one of its members—it might be a son, or a daughter, or even one of the parents?

This foolish one is the evil destiny of that family. The rest live in terror of his or her intermittent attacks upon the household peace, which cannot be prevented by any degree of vigilance or foresight, or by any amount of precaution. Nothing save death is so inevitable as the action of the fool. In fact the only law to which he or she seems amenable is the Law of Recurrence. He or she is under a fixed and fatal necessity of coming back always and repeating the deed, whatever it may be which fills that house with a sleepless fear.

A pathetic, heart-broken effort is made by the victims of the fool to keep the sad truth from the neighbors, but this never entirely succeeds. Such a household carries its own peculiar atmosphere of tragedy. The milkman has his guess and the grocer's boy could put you wise as to something queer in a certain closet. The family are not hospitable to callers and the house seems as it were in a state of siege. Something breathes therein of the tragic disunion among its members, and it is not so monstrous a fancy that the very walls seem trying to cry out! But if nothing else whispered of the secret it would be betrayed by the exuberant well-being of the fool.

For in that devoted house the fool alone has perfect health, sleeps well, eats hearty and shows no ravages of care or conscience. The others are all at peak and pine—sick from fear of the blow always suspended—knowing it will fall, yet not the less dreading it, though for the hundredth or the thousandth time. Such a fear produces horrible disorders of the nervous system in its victims. Life becomes a waking nightmare. Healthful sleep is forever banished. Yes, they are all sick from fear of the family Nemesis—a sickness for which there is *no cure but one!* And of that it is absurd to think while looking upon the frolic health of the fool.

Would not one say that there was at work here some infernal mocking spirit which personifies the very principle of evil and operates through an all but unconscious human agency? But why, oh my God, why should such a curse be permitted! . . .

Nearly all insanity comes from vice, and alienists tell us the most hopeless case is that wherein mental disease co-exists with a vigorous bodily constitution. There is some hope where body and mind are both ill, but broken brain and sound body make a combination that defies the doctor.

This truth seems to apply to the type of fool we have been considering—one who is not mad enough or wicked enough to justify the restraints of law, the padded cell or the strait-jacket. One indeed that gives scarcely any outward sign of the internal malady that makes him or her so dangerous. One who is doubtless often unconscious of the evil that he does, and who cannot see with apprehensive eye the misery he is inflicting upon those around him.

The fool, then, is an instrument—but of what? Surely of no power benign! We live in a time that sticks out the tongue at superstitions, but who that has deeply considered the matter can resist the old belief that there is some occult destiny behind the fool of a family—some ancestral sin of the blood which calls for expiation in this wise?

Again, the terror which the fool exercises in his or her little circle has the blind force of inevitable, supernatural things. It can no more be resisted than death, and to meet it with violence is as one might say to lay hands upon the body of God! . . .

Pity those—and they are not few, believe me—whose health declines, whose hopes wither, whose years pass without fruit, while they accept their fate at the hands of the family fool! I say again, one of the most tragic ironies of life. We do not hear so much of it as we should, were not the honor of families engaged to keep such histories hidden from the world.

## STYLE AND THE PUBLIC

LUCETTE writing from a far Western college poses me this problem: "Can Literature—the real classic thing—hope to hold its own in a democracy like ours?"

Which may be amplified: Has it a fighting chance with the newspapers and popular magazines, and now the "movies," all making their clamant, strenuous appeal to the common eye and mind?

I fear me much that judgment must be rendered against the Lady with the classic fillet on her hair. She will not descend from her lofty station to court the crowd, and they cannot rise to her:—the situation is clearly impossible.

Our democracy is quite unlike that of ancient Athens, where the common crowd went to hear and judge the masterpieces of Sophocles and Euripides, the orations of Pericles and Cymon. We have no hucksters and fishwives capable of correcting the speech of a philosopher. Our many-headed thing speaks a degraded dialect—the lowest and most corrupt form of speech ever used by a partly civilized people: which to copy in its literal horror is the profit of our Journalism and the ambition of no small part of our Literature.

Sizing up the contrast fairly, it is extremely difficult to believe that the Greek mob (*hoi polloi*) ever existed,—as described by the historians.

Just the other day an English critic was scolding the bad style of American writers. A very unhumorous proceeding, but it seems the Englishman never learns. It is true our writers lack style, in the classic sense—few of them aim at it, to do them justice—but that is because there is no public to demand it, or (as the publishers would say) to *pay for it.*

The tradition of style died with Hawthorne and the New England Brahmins. The crowd could not and would not read these worthies to-day: and what the crowd will not read is very difficult to publish, save at the author's personal expense. The popular magazine, intent solely upon circulation and advertising, *i. e.,* profit, was the first influence to discount style in writing. Journalism has worked to the same end, with its slipshod methods and its hatred of literature. The newspaper, the magazine, which is only a variant of the newspaper, have to a great extent displaced the book in American homes. The universal printing press gives semi-darkness, not light. Cheap literature is making us a cheap people—incapable of real knowledge, incapable of just expression, incapable of fine feeling. To talk of style for such a public—it is to laugh! Our host of literary mechanics zealously give their aid to down the hated superstition. The mark of a successful editor is recognized to be the intuition with which he avoids literary style: in the vulgar speech, it is something he would not throw at a dog!

However, the condition is a perfectly natural one, and we need not refer it to that hatred of great and exclusive excellence which is supposed to be the mark of republics. Athens *was* a republic and France is. But we have the largest *illiterate* reading public in the world: not absolutely unlettered, but unable or unwilling to read books in classical or strictly regular English. Just as all or most of our people are able to speak intelligibly, to make themselves understood orally, while only a very small fraction can do so *grammatically*. Think how few people whom you meet casually have this accomplishment. Why, I know successful authors who cannot open their mouths or write a page without doing violence to Lindley Murray (and 'tis a safe bet that they wouldn't know him from Thothmes the Third!).

Well, then: here we have an immense public to whom all print looks the same—but they prefer dialect or scrambled English, as enabling them to exercise the intellectual patronage of the uneducated. Immense too is their literary hunger, and fortunate the publisher who can give them what they want. The attempt to do this may be disastrous to the higher interests of literature, but it now and then results in a Best Seller. Howbeit, I am far from denying that a genuine talent like Whitcomb Riley or Peter Dunne or Seumas MacManus occasionally appears in the motley of dialect: of their base imitators the "less said the better."

Finally, the magazines are run to make money in the hustling American fashion, and not to foster a correct literary taste. Those who edit or conduct them are commonly a set of men to whom Walt Whitman seems the farthest thing back in literary history; who would not know Ronsard from Chatterton or a Della Cruscan from a Boston Browningite.

Read John Adams Thayer's book—the confessions of a successful magazine publisher—and you will discover (if the truth has not already dawned upon you) that literature *per se* is the most negligible proposition in the whole magazine world. The author of this book is completely successful in avoiding literary subjects. He never discusses writers or literary folk, though he has been paymaster to many of them. He is candidly of the opinion that a business manager is more important to a magazine than any editor, however gifted. But he does frankly admire one writer whose articles greatly helped the success of his publication. I refer to the shy and self-effacing Tom Lawson, whose fuliginous style, like the cloud-burst or the cyclone, seems a phenomenon peculiar to our uncultured land.

Finally, Mr. John Adams Thayer by "one satiric touch" showed his crushing contempt for American literature—he wrote a book himself! Truth compels the admission, however, that Mr. Thayer's book is vastly more amusing than the Works of Tom Lawson. . . .

Nathless, I would not deny that there be many industrious literary persons in our midst. Some can write with both hands, and others are quite expert at composing on the typewriter. But style is in the ivied grave of the Brahmins.

## THE INDEX

I HAVE just read a newspaper interview with a Catholic priest in New York regarding the attitude of the Church toward certain books of Maurice Maeterlinck's. The reverend gentleman was quoted as saying that all of Maeterlinck's literary works should be placed on the *Index Expurgatorius.*

This, as the reader may not know, is a list of books officially condemned by the Catholic Church as injurious to faith and morals, and as such, forbidden to the faithful. I do not believe that it is regarded seriously by intelligent Catholics, and its prohibitions are, I think, of a sort more honored in the breach than the observance. For to comply with the injunctions of the Index were to deprive oneself of a great part of the very best modern literature. In our day, faith would scarcely venture to incur such a handicap.

It seems that certain books of Maeterlinck's are

already on the Index (curiously enough, he was educated by the Jesuits), and that one recently so interdicted was his essay on Immortality—a beautiful piece of literature and a treasure of exquisite thought, whatever may be its shortcomings from a theological point of view.

Maeterlinck's comment upon the action of the Church in placing him under ban, was charmingly concise:—"Publisher will be delighted—otherwise only a prehistoric phenomenon of no importance!"

The incident might be used to point anew the absurdity of the whole Index-expurgatorial business and the prejudice which it needlessly excites against the old Church.

There can be no question that the Church is within its rights when it pronounces certain books dangerous to the faith or morals of its members. But such warning might be conveyed and enforced without adopting a means so offensive to modern sensibilities. The *invidia* of this proceeding of the Index, not to add its uselessness and impolicy, should long since have relegated it to the Vatican museum of antiquities.

That will surely happen one of these fine days

when a Pope comes along—perhaps an American! —who can think in terms of the Twentieth Century.

In many respects the Catholic Church is the most liberal institution in the world, else it could not be universal as it is: why does it perpetuate this stigma of ancient intolerance, this hateful taboo upon genius and thought?

The Index is a nuisance and a manufacturer of odium. It belongs with other curiosities and instruments more or less mildly corrective in the sealed-up chambers of the Inquisition.

Put the Index away! It is a reminder that the Church has sometimes mistakenly warred against light and knowledge, which might else be condoned and forgotten. It harks back to blunders that are worse than crimes. It spells Galileo and his immortal, "But it *does* move!" It furnishes an ironic note upon infallibility from which no amount of sanctified and purpled assurance can take the sting. It is a sardonic anachronism marking what has been lost rather than what has been gained. It is a reproach to the intelligent and a foolish bugaboo to the ignorant. It is a mediæval owl fluttering blinded in the full light of our day.

Christianity is beyond question the most precious moral treasure in the world, but who believes that it depends for its preservation upon the Index Expurgatorius?

The liberal Pope who is coming (most probably from America) will recognize the fatal error so long and so invidiously persisted in, of making the Church appear as a sworn enemy to intellectual power. The letter killeth! If unchangeable dogma is necessary to the eternal life of the Church, not the less is perfect freedom needed for the inspirations of genius. The compliment which a bigoted and time-worn prescription has paid to Maeterlinck will be generally regretted, and not least by open-eyed adherents of the old Church, who can discriminate between literature and dogma. But it means the finish of the Index Expurgatorius: that venerable institution is doomed to add itself to its own list of victims, and disappear without the public honors of an *auto-da-fé*.

## TWO HEROES

MR. ROOSEVELT'S biographers—a hasty crop—abetted by many journalists, are boring us again about Roosevelt's "genius," thus evincing their ignorance of the language as well as their inability to estimate the man.

Mr. Roosevelt was a genius if by that term is meant a person of strong mental capacity, energy unlimited, industry ditto, ambition extraordinary, and egotism almost without modern precedent. Genius certifies the *mens divinior,* something altogether beyond the endowment of ordinarily talented men. Can it be fairly imputed to Roosevelt? He has written many books, but they are not properly literature, and they contain not a single page illumined with that inward light that never was on sea or land. Speeches innumerable he has made—not one is become a classic. None of our Presidents equalled him in the length or number of his state papers, or the rapidity with which these have sunk into oblivion. We were always hearing about

Roosevelt's "tremendous vitality" (especially from his nonagenarian admirer, Dr. Lyman Abbott), but strangely enough, he could not impart it to his literary expression.

It is said that Mr. Roosevelt has written or dictated more words, mere words, than any other man of whom history preserves a record. A colossal proof of mediocrity!—Napoleon is every hour recalled by his apothegms—flashes of his dazzling genius—striking as his victories. That life of life which embalms the vital word was not one of Roosevelt's gifts, nor an attribute of his "genius." This man of endless verbosity has scarcely penned or uttered a single sentence that leaps from the brain at mention of his name. My own memory is more than commonly retentive of such things, and at this moment I can only recall—"Carry a big stick" and "Dear Maria." Nothing particularly orphic about these sentiments, I submit.

Think of Lincoln's immortal speeches and letters!

Roosevelt did not strike Europe as a genius, and his grand tour heralded, as Mark Twain said, by a park of artillery, failed to yield the expected results. Paris listened to him politely, while inwardly enjoying his quaint likeness to *Tartarin* (first signalized by the present writer). Berlin was neither impressed by his learning nor flattered by a certain neurotic resemblance to the Kaiser.

To be plain, Roosevelt is a monumental instance of an old American vice which has often moved the derision of Europe: I mean the absurd exaggeration of quite measurable qualities, to which we are prone as a people. Roosevelt is notable and interesting enough, however, without accepting the additions and embellishments of his fanatical admirers or the hypocritical praise of journalists to whom he was so long a first-page attraction.

I admit, however, that in the art of self-exploitation, of focussing and keeping public attention fixed upon himself—an art that was not disdained by the great Napoleon—our Teddy attained to something very like genius. It was really charlatanism, of course—but how few can discriminate here!

* * * * * *

In digging up your bones, Tom Paine,
Will Cobbett has done well:

You'll visit him on earth again,
He'll visit you in Hell!

Byron's careless epigram gives us in little the popular notion and the popular prejudice regarding one of the notables of history—he was always "Tom" Paine and hell was never far from the thought or mention of him. There has been a slight improvement in public manners, perhaps in public intelligence, since my lord penned his merry lines.

It is now conceded by good scholars that, as much as any man, Thomas Paine helped to make the United States of America. He was the literary genius of the Revolution and his burning words inspired the hearts of the people in the hours of discouragement and defeat. His phrase,—"These are the times that try men's souls"—illuminates that gigantic struggle and has become one of the shibboleths of liberty. Without Paine the success of the American Revolution is almost unthinkable, and despite the persistent effort of bigots to diminish and disparage him, his place in history is secure.

The great difference betwixt Paine and George the Third, was that the latter firmly believed in the Christian Hell and in the submission of the American colonists. Paine believed in neither and very earnestly argued against both; but it has hurt him more to deny Hell than to combat the British supremacy.

Mr. Roosevelt, who was much better educated than Paine (the latter was born poor and educated himself), has written many more books than Paine, but somehow he has never contrived to write a single phrase as memorable as the one quoted above. I believe this single phrase—"These are the times that try men's souls"—is worth all that Mr. Roosevelt has published.

In a rather unworthy way Mr. Roosevelt has associated his name with Paine by characterizing the latter in one of his books as a "dirty little atheist." This is an outrage to the Hero of the Revolution, and it furnishes a flagrant instance of Mr. Roosevelt's bad literary manners. It was also a misleading and unjust characterization. Paine was *not* dirty, *not* an atheist, and he was in stature some *five inches taller* than the Hero of Kettle Hill. It is true he was much inferior to Mr. Roosevelt in breadth of paunch and width of dental exposure; but these points are not in controversy.

## THE SHE WOLF'S MILK

NO small brother of Dante is Gabriele D'Annunzio. The milk of the She Wolf is in his veins. The old terrible Latin fire glows in his heart and brain. He is the greatest living poet of his country—it may be of the whole world.

I have lately read his "Francesca da Rimini" in the translation made by Arthur Symons—a marvelous translation, I dare avow, though I have no acquaintance with the original. Is there any English play—I do not except even the best tragedies of Shakespeare—that surpasses this in depth and intensity of passion? If there is I have no knowledge of it. The love of Romeo and Juliet seems a mere boy-and-girl flirtation compared with the fateful, flame-like, irresistible passion which leads D'Annunzio's Paolo and Francesca to their tragic end. No doubt the old play is much staled by age-long familiarity—we have seen it too often and we know the lines by heart—and Shakespeare always makes his people talk too much. The Balcony Scene is, it may be granted, the finest piece of sentimentalism ever written. On the other hand, the Tower Scene in D'Annunzio's play has, it seems to me, a more grandly conceived and intensely realized tragic value than any single episode in "Romeo and Juliet."

But making full allowance for the depreciation which time and use have visited upon Shakespeare's play, the superiority of the Italian's work, in certain respects, is still manifest. The conception of love has changed since the Elizabethans, and the modern world apprehends it as a cleaner and finer and grander thing, involving "ultimate issues" undreamed of by Shakespeare, great as was his vision. In proof of this assertion,—which I am well aware will startle many—the entire love-making of Paolo and Francesca may be cited. Who will deny that it is on a plane of passion far higher than Shakespeare gives us or seems to have understood—passion which, though glowing with the white fires of the Italianate imagination, still renders such an account of the soul's participation in the tragedy as you will vainly seek in Shakespeare? Read, in particular, the last scene of the play, with the speeches of the lovers before they are surprised and slain by the Lamester. I venture to quote, though to wrench such poetry from its context is, I feel, hardly warrantable by any excess of admiration.

PAOLO.
Come, come, Francesca! Many hours of gladness
We have before us,
With the wild melody of unknown winds
And the swift ravishment of solitude
In fire, and the violent
River without a goal,
And the immortal thirst;
But now this hour that flies
Fills me with lust to live
A thousand lives,
In the quiver of the air that kisses you,
In the short breath of the sea,
In the fury of the world,
That not one thing
Of all the infinite things
That are in you
Lie hid from me,
And I die not before I have ploughed up
Out of your depths
And relished to its infinite root in you,

My perfect joy.

(*He draws her towards the cushions by the windows.*)

FRANCESCA.

Kiss me upon my eyes, upon my brow,
Upon my cheeks, my throat,
So . . . So . . .
Stay, and my wrists, my fingers . . .
So . . . so . . . And take my soul and pour it out,
Because the breath of the night
Turns back my soul again
To things of long ago,
And the low voice of the night turns back
My soul to things that were,
And joys enjoyed are they that now weigh down
My heart, and as you were
I see you still, and not as you shall be,
My fair friend, my sweet friend.

* * *

FRANCESCA.

Here in the book, here where you have not read:
"We have been one life; it were a seemly thing
That we be also one death."

PAOLO.

Let the book

Be closed!

(*He rises, closes the book on the reading desk, and blows out the taper.*)

And read in it no more. Not there
Our destiny is written, but in the stars,
That palpitate above
As your throat palpitates,
Your wrists, your brow,
Perhaps because they were your garland once,
Your necklet when you went
Burningly through the ways of Heaven? From what
Vineyard of earth were these grapes gathered in?
They have the smell
Or drunkenness and honey,
They are like veins, they are swollen with delight,
Fruits of the night! The flaming feet of Love
Shall tread them in the winepress. Give me your mouth,
Again! Again!

Is the sense of inevitable fate giving a sharper edge to desire, a more imperative rule and a more tragic value to passion, anywhere in Shakespeare more strongly manifest than in the closing scenes of this play? I found myself *fearing to come to an end* of the book—a rare experience for a time-hardened reader!

Again I dare avow that if there be anything in English dramatic literature that will sustain an adequate comparison with D'Annunzio's tragedy of Francesca da Rimini, in the respects above noted, I am not acquainted with the work.

## BORROW

THE name of George Borrow has a certain pleasing flavor, a specious currency in the mouths of the bookishly inclined, though it may be doubted whether his work is equally familiar to them, or whether he is in active requisition as an extant author. Something of his "airy fame" is due to the kindly references of better known authors like R. L. S., and there the incurious or unrecondite reader is apt to leave it. I have therefore been a little surprised to see his "Lavengro" listed recently with a collection of sturdy English classics and offered under the imprint of an American publisher.

This book of Borrow's is certainly not a true classic, though it may be accredited to a place amongst the Curiosities of Literature, like the elder Disraeli's neglected work of that title, now itself a curiosity.

I have never been able to get through Borrow's

book, in spite of a strong taste for picaresque literature. The author always talks me to sleep in a chapter or so. He is too much the pedant, and a self-made pedant at that, to tell a good story. There are only one or two readable episodes in the entire book—perhaps just one, the fight in Mumper's Dingle; while the merit even of this has been much exaggerated. By the way, Borrow is at least notable for his attitude toward and admiration of that declining institution, the British Prize Ring, so long reputed among the glories of England. He was something of a pugilist himself—did he not beat the Flaming Tinman?—and in his literary practice he seems to betray the manners of the squared circle.

For the rest, his "Lavengro" is without art and lacks even the sort of vulgar interest that usually attaches to the chronicles of bagmen. No writer ever talked so much about himself with so slight a warrant; the reader perforce moves away from him as from an importunate beggar. He has neither true learning, nor style, nor story, nor valuable observation, nor philosophy of life. His besetting dread of Jesuitry and the Romish Church is worthy of a Devonshire peasant in the days of

Monmouth. Finally, he appears to me not so much a shallow scoundrel as what is worse, a dull and pragmatic one. To see Borrow in a company of genuine classics is like seeing a flunky in masquerade as a gentleman. One's obvious duty is to show him the door.

To these strictures it is no answer to point the continued life of Borrow's books. Many dull or stupid books, deemed useful in the English literary tradition, are kept alive by the practice of publishers. Besides, has it not occurred to you that stupid people require stupid books and their patronage is not to be slighted? *Chacun à son goût!*—think you Barabbas is in trade singly for his health or from the love of pure literature? . . . I merely contend that "Lavengro" is not eligible for a collection of classics.

However, there is one memorable passage in "Lavengro" which goes far towards qualifying my disparagement of Borrow, and in which the accent of literature makes itself heard, clear and triumphant. It has curiously been ignored by those persons who wrote and published so copiously on the centenary of Byron. I refer to the striking page or two wherein he describes the funeral of Lord Byron which he himself witnessed as a tramp in the streets of London. The contrast between himself, poor and nameless, yet conscious of latent power, and the dead man passing by in the double glory of rank and fame,—a poet without a peer, a peer among poets,—snatches from his heart words of a bitter eloquence that long stamp the memory. He is not just to Byron, of course, and he speaks as a Pariah might of a Brahmin, with envy that deepens to cordial hatred. Nevertheless, the short passage, as literature, is to my mind worth the rest of his book.

## BROWNING

WAS there ever such a deformed talent as Browning's—a genuine talent, too, though weakened and handicapped by a most irritating self-consciousness and a repulsive literary method? Heine said that Victor Hugo's genius had a hump, like his own *Quasimodo:* Browning's would seem to have had a bad case of *locomotor ataxia.* Never a poet of occasional inspiration did so much bad work: that a strong man should have wasted a long life in such futile employment is truly a dispiriting thought.

And Browning did even worse than this: he set up and consecrated a legend of knock-kneed verse, mere verbal obfuscation and orphic stupidity, which is still exerting its noxious influence. In strict fact both Robert Browning and Elizabeth Barrett Browning took a fall out of poetry from which it has never recovered. Their enormous production, their cloying sentimentalism, and the cult of both set up by the half-baked Della Cruscans of England and America, are still to be reckoned potent causes in the poetical depression of our time. "Thank God," said Fitzgerald, "that there will be no more *Aurora Leighs!*" Who that loves poetry does not thank God that there will be no more *Asolandos* and *Red Cotton Nightcap Countries*, and other grotesque progeny of the Browning imagination? The wonder is that he could now and then achieve true art, in the midst of his puerile or monstrous conceptions.

Staggering remains the output of that belabored fancy of Browning's, daunting to readers and poets alike. A poet should write for the future, but he should not pile Pelion upon Ossa as Browning did, to overwhelm and discourage it. Browning and bathos!—the end was inevitable. Now the sentimentalists will not like to hear this, but there is the undeniable fact that their adored Brownings have done more than all the poets good and bad of the last century to confirm and extend the public hatred of poetry.

## TRELAWNY

TRELAWNY tells us in his "Recollections of Byron and Shelley," how he saw the corpse of Byron at Missolonghi, and how he sent Fletcher out of the room in order that he might gratify his curiosity to have a look at the feet. Under the circumstances, one feels that no man of his quality ever told a more detestable thing about himself. But this by the way. Trelawny says *both feet were clubbed,* and I believe he either lied, from a desire to exaggerate the mystery and from his ill-disguised hatred * of Byron, or perhaps blundered from a real confusion; he admits that Fletcher returning suddenly surprised him in his ghoulish inspection.

That Trelawny falsified or blundered or perverted the facts, the following obvious consideration, which yet seems not to have occurred to the critics, leaves little doubt. He was always curious

* Byron used to say that Trelawny set himself to look the part of the "Corsair" after reading his (Byron's) poem of that title.

about Byron's lameness, and refers to the matter several times in an invidious way. But why did he have to wait for Byron's death to discover the actual facts of the deformity? On his own showing, he was admitted to the most familiar intercourse with him—indeed, he represents himself as rather evading Byron's importunate hospitalities. Under these conditions, a man would find it difficult to conceal *two club feet* as effectually as a strawberry mark in his armpit! Yet Byron seems to have baffled Trelawny's keen and hostile curiosity until death gave the latter his sinister opportunity.

Above all, Trelawny relates that he frequently bathed and swam long distances in the sea with Byron. He is at pains to make himself out the better (or stronger) swimmer, and he plainly discloses his jealous emulation. A fin, he says, is better than a foot for swimming, scornfully alluding to the poet's disability: still he omits to tell us that he discovered anything in the circumstances. Did Byron wear, even while swimming, the elaborate foot-gear intended to hide or attenuate his deformity? The notion is ridiculous—it would have hopelessly hindered him. And if he did wear it, would Trelawny have failed to observe and report the fact? Assuredly not. I conclude, therefore, that he drew upon his imagination when many years afterward he sat down to transcribe his "recollections" of the great poet. Trelawny was then a soured and broken man, a partisan, like his crony Leigh Hunt, of the literary faction that sought to degrade the name and fame of Byron. His witness will never be accepted by the fairminded.

Trelawny seems to have been a marplot at best, and poor Shelley might have lived out his days, had he not had the ill luck to fall in with him. Manifestly, he encouraged Shelley in those seafaring hazards for which the latter was so grotesquely unfitted, and which cost him his life.

This book of Trelawny's, without literary art, blunt and outspoken like the man himself, is disfigured by obvious spite and prejudice as regards Lord Byron. Interest in it was revived by the centenary of both poets nearly synchronizing (1822 and 1824), though oddly enough, no edition has appeared for many years and the book is become a rarity. But it seems destined to live by virtue of a few vivid first-hand impressions of the greatest poet, the most striking literary personality of his age; while it is scarcely less memorable for what it has to record of Shelley.

In particular, Trelawny's picture of the last days at Casa Magni, the drowning of Shelley in the Gulf of Spezia and the cremation of his body on the seashore, at which Byron assisted, is one of enduring value—better even than the more meditated, consciously artful description of Leigh Hunt. It was indeed a tragedy which no literary art could heighten.

It should in fairness be added that Trelawny's account, in this same book, of his own adventures (following Byron's death) in the war between Turks and Greeks, is of great interest and leaves a more favorable impression of the "Corsair" than his ill-judged efforts to settle the comparative literary status of Byron and Shelley. An attempt to assassinate him that failed only by a hair's breadth, reveals the stern mettle of the man. Shot from behind and several heavy bullets lodged in his back, he pulled through by virtue of his iron constitution, and lived many years thereafter, though but as a shadow of the old gallant "Tre." I have stood by his grave which is near that of Shelley in the Protestant Cemetery at Rome. One ends by admiring that perfect devotion, nay worship! which even in death would not be separated from its idol.

# AMOURETTES

ARTHUR SCHNITZLER has been called the Austrian Maupassant because his *forte* is the erotic short story. He seems to have founded himself upon the French *conteur* as regards this specialty, which he has adapted very successfuly to the processes of the German mind. It is remarkable enough that of all the writers "influenced" by Maupassant and more or less consciously following in his footsteps, this Austrian should have come nearest to rivaling the Master. Needless to say, he is an artist in his own right, else the world would not have complimented him upon his likeness to the author of "Boule de Suif."

But the likeness is no great matter, when all is said, and it is founded chiefly upon a similarity of technique. In this respect it may well be asked, who has not learned something from the pupil of Flaubert? Schnitzler doubtless owes to Maupassant his comparative dexterity among German writers in his handling of the short story. But he has not touched upon the heart of the Frenchman's secret—that remains, in its full potency, a thing which will not be seen again. The writer who, as Henry James said, found short cuts in the night, has nothing to fear from those who would borrow his name.

It is rather in his unlikeness to Maupassant that I find Schnitzler interesting. The Frenchman's trick of telling a story in which the dynamic effect is infallibly calculated, like a marksman who can always be counted on to ring the bull's-eye—the stern preparedness with which he sets about the work, brushing away unessentials with that powerful gesture of his—the literal transcription of life, as it seems, which is yet the selective miracle of art—that style so sternly simple, so incomparably terse, yet vibrant with personality like a stretched bow in the wind—that faculty, in which he is still unrivaled, of adequately presenting a passion or a tragedy within a dozen pages—that dolorous though morbid sympathy with the miseries of life, which remains like an unhealed wound with the reader when Hugo's sentimentalism is forgotten—that for the most part unjoyous mirth of the humorist who never laughs—these are the stigmata of the Frenchman's talent which the Austrian cannot be said to have made his own. It does not seem to me that, more than a half-dozen writers who might readily be named, he suggests any of these traits at their full value.

But he has positive merits, without regard to his alleged copying of Maupassant, and these are effectively disclosed in the volume entitled "Viennese Idylls." Like the Frenchman, he is all too preoccupied with the sexual passion, but with finer restraint and delicacy. His love affairs are *amourettes* and seldom lead to tragic conclusions: —however they do sometimes, and then his power deepens (as in "The Farewell"), revealing the stern artist behind the graceful *conteur*. Schnitzler is an elegant sensualist, and his favorite theme is the *liaison*, but he orders the matter with more sentiment than the too realistic author of "Bel-Ami"—(Have I not said that he is a German?). It is the same dish, *bien entendu*, but the sauce is different.

Maupassant undresses his mistress for you and gives you the peculiar odor of her nude flesh.

Schnitzler brings you some flowers to smell which she wore in her breast the night she left her lover after a quarrel. The favorite theme of both involves a perpetual violation of the Sixth Commandment, but even in going thus far Schnitzler does less violence to conventional ideas. He is profoundly immoral, of course, but still a German sentimentalist and very respectable withal. Most of his amorous intrigues have to do with persons of the Viennese aristocracy, who behave very properly in their boldest acts of impropriety. Somehow Schnitzler's stories convey the notion that lapses of a sexual nature are effectively condoned by good manners and social position in the transgressors.

This is an added bait to the sexual motive, and indeed Schnitzler may almost claim the liaison *comme il faut* as an original invention. Herein, at least, he owes little or nothing to Maupassant—whose essays in kind are on an inferior plane, and mostly referable to the period of his decadence. The air of good breeding and graceful aristocratic velleity, which the Austrian has managed to throw about these light-o'-loves that pair and unpair with smiling politeness and unwounded hearts, like the figures in a dance, is not to be reckoned an achievement of the Frenchman's, too much given as he was to *le mot Gaulois.*

I may here remark that tales of aristocratic venery have always had a strong fascination for the public. Witness the perennial popularity of certain memoirs of royal concubines and mistresses, which, on account of the fat price they always fetch. remain the "velvet" of the publishing trade. Look at "The Red Lily" by Anatole France, which has had, especially in the English translation, a hundred readers to one for any other work of the same author. No need to ask why, if you have read the book, steeped in a gracious and refined immorality, which, if extensively copied in society at large would lead us back to arboreal man.

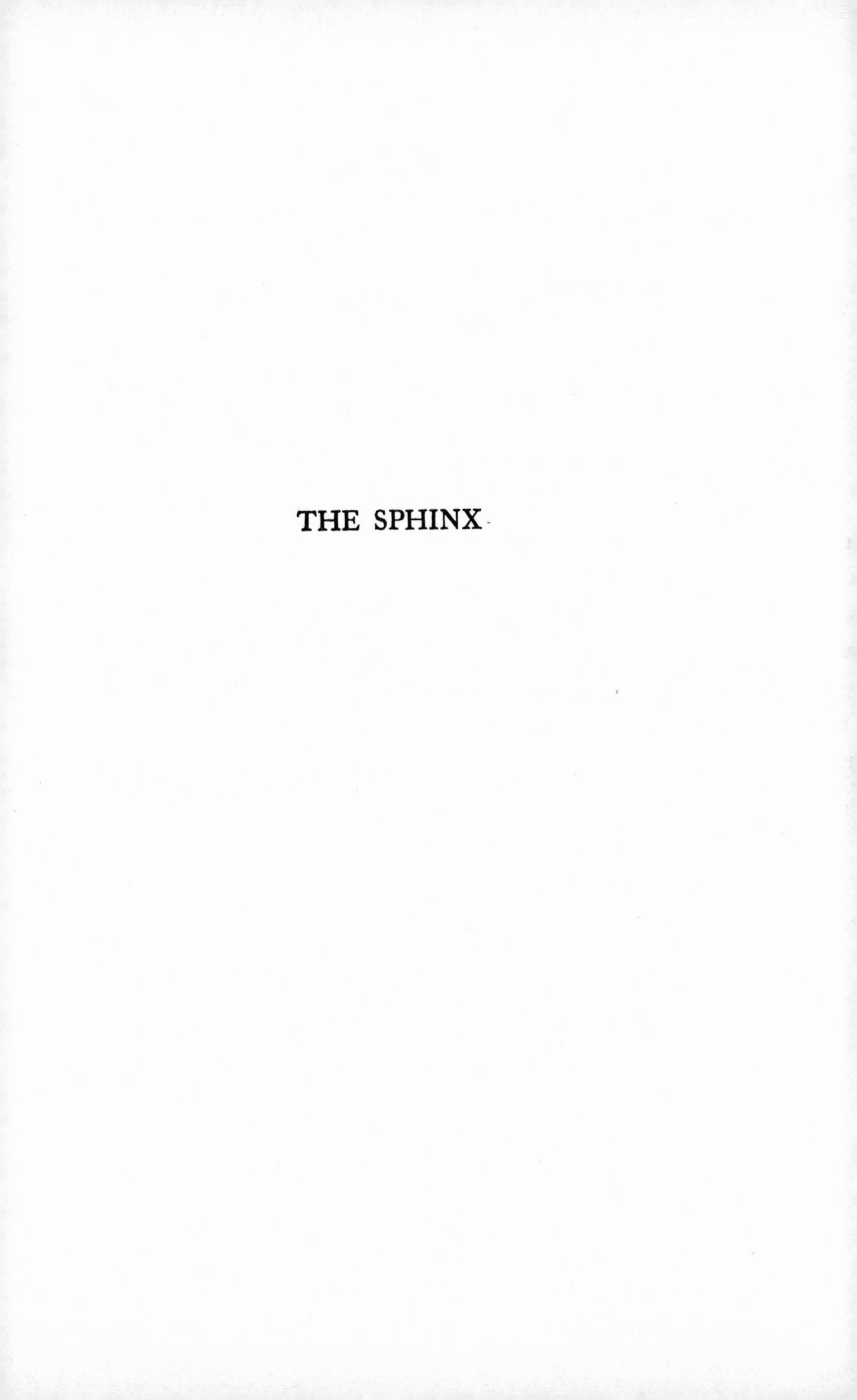

THE SPHINX

# THE SPHINX

## I—THE ETERNAL DUEL

LOVE is the one illusion with which we gladly cheat ourselves unto the end.

LIFE and love lure us constantly, with an ultimate purpose to destroy.

THE voice of a loving and beloved woman singing in the house—there's a poem without words!

WE are never more faithful than when we are about to betray.

THE woman rarely has power herself, but she serves man as an instrument or means to power.

IN hate as in love people understand each other very well without words.

THE angels of our youth often, alas! turn into fat women; but, on the other hand, fat women seem to take an unconscionable time about turning into angels.

THE woman who tells you that she wants to be loved for her soul as well as her body, has probably had more experience of the latter.

THERE is a French saying that woman must either love or hate. She can do both, too, at the same time. Some men prefer it that way and labor to that end, but it is very wearing.

THERE is such a thing in marriage as fidelity of the body and infidelity of the soul. Religion would rather have it that way than divorce—and likewise the Devil!

STRANGE to say, love is sometimes born after a season of hatred, and then it is in truth a terrible passion, full of remorse and insatiable tenderness.

IF I could have but one heart true to me in every thought and pulse I should count myself happier than any king that ever wore a crown. But I should fear my kingdom more than the sovereignty of Alexander.

A MAN'S climacteric usually occurs about the time he has to look after his health; a woman's when her emotions have ceased to be dangerous.

THERE are infidelities of the soul which wound more deeply and estrange more hopelessly than those of the flesh. Virtuous women are much given to them.

IF thou truly lovest, thou canst not be absent from the Beloved nor she from thee. Let there be only room for thy heart to beat in the darkness—she is *there!*

I COULD easily have enough fame and fortune to content me, but never, never could I have enough of love!

A HOUSE divided against itself offers to the Devil his most congenial loafing place.

AT twenty-five not to be able to get enough of

each other; at fifty to dread each other's touch—that is the end of many a romance.

WHERE love once has been you shall not pass off something else instead. This is a deception that never obtains without the implied consent of both parties.

A CHARMING woman complains that I do not understand her at all. Of course, I don't—show me the man who thinks he understands a woman, and I will show you the perfect fool.

NATURE is the most cruel of jesters and she has invented nothing worse than that delusion of the senses which lasts until two beings are made wretched for life.

SHAKESPEARE tells us that a low soft voice is an excellent thing in woman, but the experience of many men argues that it can be no rarity in hell!

YES, dearie, my mistake always has been to set my loves and friendships too high, whence I have

suffered some cruel disillusions and am indeed ever bleeding from the same cause. But I am not sure that I would have it otherwise. Every perfect joy casts a shadow, and when love is gone there are at least our wounds to kiss.

I ONCE knew a philosopher who would contend that woman's virtue was a quality invented by men for their pleasure, convenience and protection.

TRUST a woman while she loves you; a man while he has reason to fear you.

NO one ever dared to accuse God of immodesty, and yet He wrote the enduring Poem of the Sexes.

THERE is one evil thing in this world which the Devil allows that he cannot improve—hate that has once been love!

BEAUTY is a very desirable thing in your wife, but don't forget that it has to be paid for, to the last drachma. He sleeps well that gladly turns away from the face on his pillow.

EXTREMES meet and love passes into hate, hate passes into love. Ah, happy they who neither love nor hate!

LOVE without calculation is the glory and disaster of youth.

A PROPER degree of passion snuffs your candle for you; too much consumes it.

THERE is an unchastity of the soul that is far worse than what is called the unchastity of the body. I have known people to be possessed of the first like a scourge of devils, who would rather die than yield to the second.

THERE is one story which the world will always refuse to believe—that of the man who passed through life without loving anyone.

THE happiest of men were he who could gather the flowers of love without the thorns. But the earth still waits for him.

I WAS at quarrel with One, and I burned to defend myself. "Fool!" said a voice within me, "dost thou

think it would be of any avail if her heart did not plead for thee? Then speak not at all, but leave thy cause to silence—and her heart!"

WE perish by our passions, but we *will* have them, though a grinning Death stand visibly behind.

THE marriage of bodies, not souls—tell me the Devil has ever found a better card than this!

THE warmth of one true heart is enough to keep the world from freezing about us.

WOMAN'S chastity is man's greatest invention, says a French cynic. And—it may be added—his most enduring superstition.

THE artistic life does not mate well with connubial exemplariness—it demands more potent stimulants than the syrupy cordial of domestic virtue. As a rule the world is apt to have a low opinion of a genius who is conspicuously faithful to his wife.

A SECOND passion is much rarer than the novelists pretend. Most men and women are used up by their first.

IMPORTANT difference between the sexes: The woman who wrongs her husband in the way that commonly justifies divorce, always hates him—she really has to! But in the reverse case the man is not at all apt to hate the woman. Is this because Nature has made the obligation of chastity more binding upon the female partner?

THE love affairs of the young furnish the conventional stuff of fiction and the drama; the passions of the old and middle-aged the real tragedies of life. Balzac's perception of this truth (which conventionality and hypocrisy blink at) did much to make him the greatest novelist of the world.

WOMAN lives wholly in and for the present; she can not suffer for the future—for a reward she may not live to taste. So she fears and distrusts the Ideal, unless it be of the accepted sort that is translatable into comfort, clothes and recognition. Nothing is rarer than a true woman idealist.

MARRIAGE is a feud, said Balzac, and in his own case the feud seems to have begun with the honeymoon, long as those lovers had waited for their bliss. But is marriage really a feud? I guess yes . . . if you don't look out!

VENERY is one of the great wasting forces of the world by which the audit of humanity is regulated; that gate through which life enters is the same by which much life goes out. It may well be symbolized by the Sphinx that devours all who cannot solve her enigma.

## SAYINGS OF SHADRACH THE WISE

MY son, if you do not chase *her,* she will chase you; and if she will not chase you, then you had better go chase yourself.

LIKEWISE beware the Skirt that fleeth when no man pursueth, for the chances are she is only trying to start something.

FORGET not, my son, that a pair of soulful Eyes, a soft and clinging Palm, and a mouth like Cupid's bow are often the lure of a Cold Proposition.

AFTER forty open your Rabelais—but don't forget that persons of middle age are very liable to skulduddery!

## II—THE DROP OF INK

NO man was ever competent to write the history of his own soul.

UNLESS ye become as little children ye shall not enter the Kingdom of Art.

TO the writer: Nothing is old, nothing is new, everything has to be said over again,—unless you catch yourself in the act!

TO an aspiring young author: One good test of the literary vocation is, if it seems more necessary for you to write than to be published.

I HAVE scarcely ever penned an article but someone told me it was of my best, and some other that it was of my worst. In my own heart I felt pretty sure that it was neither.

TO have nothing to say and to say it at all hazards, passes for much that is called achievement in literature.

STRINDBERG is the Schopenhauer of the drama—his drama, like his name, sets the teeth on edge.

PUSH and hustle are the Gog and Magog of the great American people, and we have cultivated these qualities to the point that we can make a success of anything, no matter how unworthy. To succeed among us, not seldom is the disgraceful thing; while failure is often a brevet of honor.

I USED to think that Thirty-five was the great age for writing and thinking men, when they should be at their ripest and best. But it seems to me now that Fifty-five (or a shade over) has certain points of superiority. Bless me, how unstable we are in our opinions!

DR. MAVERICK BRANDER laments in heart-rending tones the over-production of literature or rather printed matter in this country. Meantime the gentleman continues to publish a couple of volumes yearly which might—oh, really might—be dispensed with. "Physician, heal thyself."

THE writer who has never known a day of defeat at his desk has never known a day of real victory.

THE main difficulty of writing is to say anything that is not an obvious quotation.

AS to women poets in general, I should say that poetry is the male principle. Departures from this rule come under the head of sexual anomalies.

THAT which is well done shall always have leave to come back and console thee.

WHY does a writer love his public? Because he has not a friend in the world to whom he can address himself with such ease and power, and with such a perfect assurance of being appreciated and understood.

I OBSERVE that nothing gives a man such real pleasure as having turned the corner in his work.

LITERATURE and the Bargain Counter have kissed—they were making a "best seller!"

IN literature the sapient public would rather converse with a living ass than with a dead lion.

THE rival whom a genuine writer most fears is himself at his best.

TO reach the sources of power, you must *break into yourself!* There they are, locked and sealed, accessible only to the supreme effort of courage and will.

THE supreme effects of genius are achieved without conscious art and seem to be more the work of nature than of the man.

NO doubt the same creative qualities go to the making of fine poems as of fine children. But it is permitted unto few men and fewer women to make both.

"I AM never ill when I write," said Emerson, but he neglected to add that he was commonly ill until his writing fit began (Mrs. Emerson could have told you). The unsealing of thought is a true birth, and birth is never without pain. This explains the artistic temperament with its feverish fits and starts, its whim and inconsistency. Through sickness to health is the Calvary of the Idea.

IF I were asked to name the one quality in which Balzac has perhaps excelled all writers, I should say: courage! Think of the bravery that went to the making of Hulot in *Cousine Bette*—the one consistent portrait of a man, equally true in Art and Nature, to be found in a hundred years of fiction.

A REVIEWER of one of my books writing in the London "Academy," professes not to understand the phrase "ranking quality." This is offered as an agreeable proof that ignorance of the English language is not strictly confined to American writers.

POETRY is essentially a more artificial method of expression than prose, and hence the public hatred of it, save in the form of songs or ballads. Few people—even few poets—care to read poetry, but there is prevalent a great hypocrisy as to this matter, since to confess so much would seem to limit one's claims to culture and literary taste.

MOST people are afraid of pure literature, that is to say, the best thought. They prefer books about books, diluters and intermediaries, the terraces to the mountain tops.

PUBLISHING is more and more an industry; authorship less and less an art.

TRUTH lies in a well and originality at the bottom of your inkpot.

YOU can not open your mouth or trace a line to express an opinion without hurting somebody. Is a man to go through the world voiceless for that?

GLORY is the sun of the dead, says Balzac. Even Shakespeare has nothing so fine.

'TIS the arch malice of fate that death or decadence always comes at the moment when men are about to seize the secret of life.

THE literary man always most directly in the public eye is the fellow who writes about the fellow who wrote a book that the majority of people haven't time or inclination to read.

JOB is a fairly popular writer and he lived some little time before the Hoe press and the Linotype. These and similar boasted inventions have added nothing to original thought, while they have infinitely increased the production of literary punk.

I HATE the man who tells me that he knows just what I would think, or say, or write, on a given occasion—yes, though he were my dear friend! Shall he, in Hamlet's phrase, pluck out the heart of my mystery? Shall he so easily plumb depths that I have not myself fathomed? Am I then so shallow a copy of himself? Is my thought of so little worth? Indeed, indeed, sir, but you shall not buy me so cheap!

TO the writer: Read enougn out not too much; no book will ever bring you the waters of that secret fountain within yourself.

TAKE heed, O writer, not to save thy thought too exclusively for posterity; the present is also to be wooed if thou wouldst win the future.

### III—FRIENDSHIP'S GARLAND

STRIKE a man anywhere but in his self-love and he will forgive you; all other wounds heal over night.

IN friendship as in love the finest fruits are gathered by those who know the value of moderation and restraint.

A MAN never tells the whole truth about himself; the Ego will not be confessed to its disadvantage.

IT is more agreeable to be loved than feared for your talent, but you will get more advantage from the latter.

YOUNG men appeal to friendship; older men to self-interest. Age is a sloughing of the generous virtues.

TWO things you should carefully avoid—the jealousy of an old man and the friendship of one too young.

HATRED of an idea may be noble; of a man is almost necessarily ignoble and degrading. One may break absolutely with a man and yet not hate him. Indeed I am still fond of one or two men between whom and myself there is no chance of reconciliation this side the grave.

EVERY soul is a mystery to every other soul. This is the Law of Spirit. You can touch the body and the intelligence,—that which we call the mind,—but the soul eludes your utmost vigilance and effort. God has set this barrier betwixt His creatures to mark the realm that belongs to Him alone.

AFTER long years made dolorous by slavery of the Spirit and the forced submission of the Mind, a bright moment dawned when I cried aloud for joy—"Thank God, I am free at last!" Then came One who sought to bind me with silken fetters that held as tightly as the old chains—it was Friendship!

INSIST on yourself, says Emerson. But first be sure of yourself; for this is the law of the suicide of the weak and the salvation of the strong.

IT may not always be true that (as the French say) there is something agreeable to us in the misfortunes of our friends. But certain it is that the unlooked-for death of an old friend causes us to cling with an almost painful affection to life.

ROCHEFOUCAULD said that Love was like the ghost of popular legend—everybody talked about it, but nobody had ever really seen it. Had the Frenchman said *Fidelity,* he would have strengthened his epigram.

PERHAPS the one thing that never happens in this world is, to find two friends or lovers who do not contrive to deceive each other.

WHO so cold and alien to thee as the hot Friend thou didst cherish over the Cup?

IT is hard to lose a friend, but it would be worse to prove false to your own guiding genius. As Stevenson said: No capitulation!

MEN are united more by their vices than their virtues, observed Balzac. It is also true that they are more closely bound by their failures than their successes. How a man will love you if you have fallen down like himself, when perhaps you should both have won out, were there any real stuff in you!

## IV—MORE OR LESS ORPHIC

NOTHING so surely punishes us as a betrayed ideal.

THE poorest of men is he who has only money in his thoughts.

TIME would get along faster but for the grudges in his pack.

FATE acts from within—no exterior force can harm you!

THE secret of continued power is that you shall not share your soul's orbit with another.

PITY the man whose dead lie not in their resting graves but live on to trouble his heart!

I AM the merriest man in the world and I am also the saddest—I could not be the one without the other. I laugh till I cry and I cry till I laugh again. This is not really a riddle—but you might ask *Touchstone.*

I HAVE never written a letter that afforded me so much satisfaction as one or two I did not write.

NATURE hears no cry for mercy and answers no flag of distress.

LIFE is so interesting—living such a tiresome business!

THE cry of old Goriot,—"We bring our children into the world and they send us out of it,"—is one of those tragic truths for which we hate the man who utters it. But truth, very truth!

DOCTORS never confess, but sometimes there's nothing like a wrong diagnosis for giving the patient a fresh hold on life.

MANY people seem to regard it as a form of

Christian charity to leave their revenges to Time —and expect him to make good.

TO say that a man is cunning is to say that he is unscrupulous, for craft would be useless if handicapped with scruples. And yet to say that a man lacks cunning is to brand him as a fool,—as the world goes.

THE mind, like the body, gets used to, and loves its chains. Men are still known to refuse liberty for the one as well as the other.

IF you think you have a bit of talent, don't go chasing after ultra-clever people—show it off where it will count for something. There is a certain economy in casting pearls before swine.

SENILITY is more to be feared than extinction. "Let not my flame lack oil to be the snuff o' younger spirits."

TO be simple, candid, honest, brave, one should have either the fortune of a prince or the wallet of a beggar.

NO matter how poor you may be, there is a thing all men are eager to take from you—your individuality!

RELIGION and Common Sense could never keep house were it not for their sister Morality.

DO not confound cunning with ability,—a too common error. A very cunning man is seldom a really able one—cunning is chiefly used as a cloak for defects.

EVERY journey's end is welcome, even that of Life.

## V—LE GRAND PEUT-ÊTRE

IF God is our Father, who is our Mother?

THE gods fade one after another, and the Universe refuses to tell its secret.

NO theologian has ever yet taken out a caveat on the Religion of Cheerfulness.

AFTER every terrible temptation the soul is conscious of God walking in the garden.

PROHIBITION scored its first failure in the Garden of Eden, and it has continued a failure even unto this day.

ONE cannot think of death as absolute while the universe survives.

THE Church married Poverty, but Wealth was the child of their nuptials.

TOO much of the flesh drives us back upon the spirit; too much of the spirit drives us out to the flesh.

THAT God himself suffered for men, is the supreme egoism of humanity and hence the one enduring religion.

WE are incredulous of death, though it be in the same house with us.

"HAD I the power," said Ingersoll, "I would make health as contagious as disease." Theologically, this sentiment alone was enough to damn him.

THE end of the world will be at hand when no heart shall say to itself: To-morrow!

WHILE men are men, religion will never be separated from those temporal interests which forever shut out the Kingdom of Heaven

HORACE prayed for an old age without baseness and not lacking the inspiration of poetry. This was the prayer of a pagan, and it has not been bettered in many centuries of Christianity.

EMERSON, whilst he lived and wrote, excited more interest than the churches. But there are always churches and an Emerson appears only once in the course of ages.

THE late Goldwin Smith passed into the Unknown with a perfectly open mind. It takes courage to do this now, and not so long ago the process was described as damnation.

THE Priest stands outside his Church and looks

at me as I come along. I had thought to go in, but now I must pass by—that one look of his turns the Church into a Prison!

I AM willing to admit that men soon sink into swine without religion that makes them accountable for their bodies as well as their souls.

THERE is no enmity, however bitter, that a man will not forget with the passing years. Yet we are asked to believe in a God of eternal hate.

DR. GOLDWIN SMITH observes that while the beavers have shown a remarkable instinct for co-operation they have never formed a church. Perhaps because there is nothing in the history of these sagacious animals to correspond to the Fall of Man.

THE Abbé Loisy, having suffered the Major Excommunication, retires to the country and goes to raising chickens. This is excellent and truly philosophic, for the raising of chickens will perhaps outlast the business of issuing Major and Minor Excommunications.

MOMUS was the Latin god of mirth, and Mercury played tricks on gods and mortals, and there were other waggish deities on Olympus. But it is not recorded that Jehovah ever laughed, nor is it written that Jesus his Son ever smiled. The fact is enormously significant, and it has had a terrible influence upon human history.

THE secrets of Heaven are well kept, says Emerson. With a million signaling spires and a host of priests posing as the familiars of Deity, no authentic message ever comes from without. God is within ourselves.

WHEN it shall be recognized that we are all sons of God no man will need to button his collar behind in order to get himself identified.

I BELIEVE that God has a sense of humour, though it cannot be proved out of the Bible. I had rather laugh than weep with my God.

# L'ENVOI

## FAREWELL TO MY BOOKS

*(For George Gordon Moore)*

## FAREWELL TO MY BOOKS

AND must we part forever, O my books,
That long have cheered me with your silent looks,
And bid me lift my head when hope was low,
And fanned the spark of thought to brighter glow,
And giv'n me of your solace evermore,
Your treasured wisdom and your varied lore—
Leave me at length when life wanes short and cold,
And take away from me the fairy gold
I still have sought in you—nor all in vain—
No, 'tis not true—let me hear that again!

Oh what a pang when my poor walls lie bare,
Where even now your ranks familiar were,
And I alone, without the host of friends
Who needs must leave me as the night impends!
Why this defection? Is there none to tell?
Have I not loved and served you but too well,
Paying the price to high allegiance given,

And holding naught in rank with you save Heaven!
Companions—comforters, can it be true
That I am called to bid farewell to you?
The Lares weep to see you pass the door,
And Fate cries out that you return no more!

Sure we have heard the wintry tempests howl
For many a year—heard too the wolf a-prowl
About the door—but poverty ne'er daunted
The heart your magic had but once enchanted.
Blackhaired was I and in youth's fiery zone
When first I made my vows to you alone,
And watched my vigil stern, e'en as a knight
Who consecrates his valiance to the right;
And now, with snowy head, my heart is yet the same
That your great voices roused to dream of fame:
Still haunted by the Vision and the Dream,
And tho' the sands run low, still following the
Gleam.
Have I not kept the faith?—O my old friends,
Do you forsake me as the night descends?

Ah, 'tis too much—you were my only wealth,
Mainspring of life itself, true source of health,
Balm for all hurts and cure for every sorrow,

In darkest hours a promised bright To-morrow.
You were the only world I cared to know,
Aye, but to keep you, did the rest forego,
To live with you the chosen of all ages,
My noble poets, heroes, warriors, sages,
Peers of immortal mind, great masters all,
Who lift us to your height e'en by your potent
thrall.
From you was all my strength—like Prospero,
Reft of my books, there's naught for me below;
And Caliban shall rule the magic Isle,
And all the charming cease, and God refuse to
smile!
Well, 'tis but a single cup to drink—and now,
The hemlock quaffed, I bear a calmer brow.

Adieu, my books!—yours is a happier fate
Than your old comrade's, left disconsolate:
Not to be scattered on the winds of trade,
A prey to chance and evil fortune made;
For you will harbor in a lofty house,
And fill the station there a Master kind allows.
Nor will he put your simple weeds to blush,
By lodging you near rivals rich in plush,

To humble you with snobbish leer and stare,
As wond'ring what your antecedents were.
The Ruby's worth is not a thing apart
From the soft flame that flickers at her heart:
Beloved estrays of many an ancient stall,
Yours is a virtue that outshines them all.

My books, I send you forth to honor meet,
Since your new Master gives you welcome sweet,
And he is ripe for all you can impart,
Lord of the fellowship of mind and heart;
And he will shelter you in his own room,
Where you shall live, as with a brighter bloom,
In kindred love and tendance—while e'en there
Your ancient lover shall at times repair,
And lay his hands upon you in fond sign
Of love that knows nor change nor slow decline;
Or human-wise, sigh for life's dwindled store,
For battles lost and won—for hopes that are no
more!